# Fantastic Faces Coloring Book

# Color Test Page

# Color Test Page

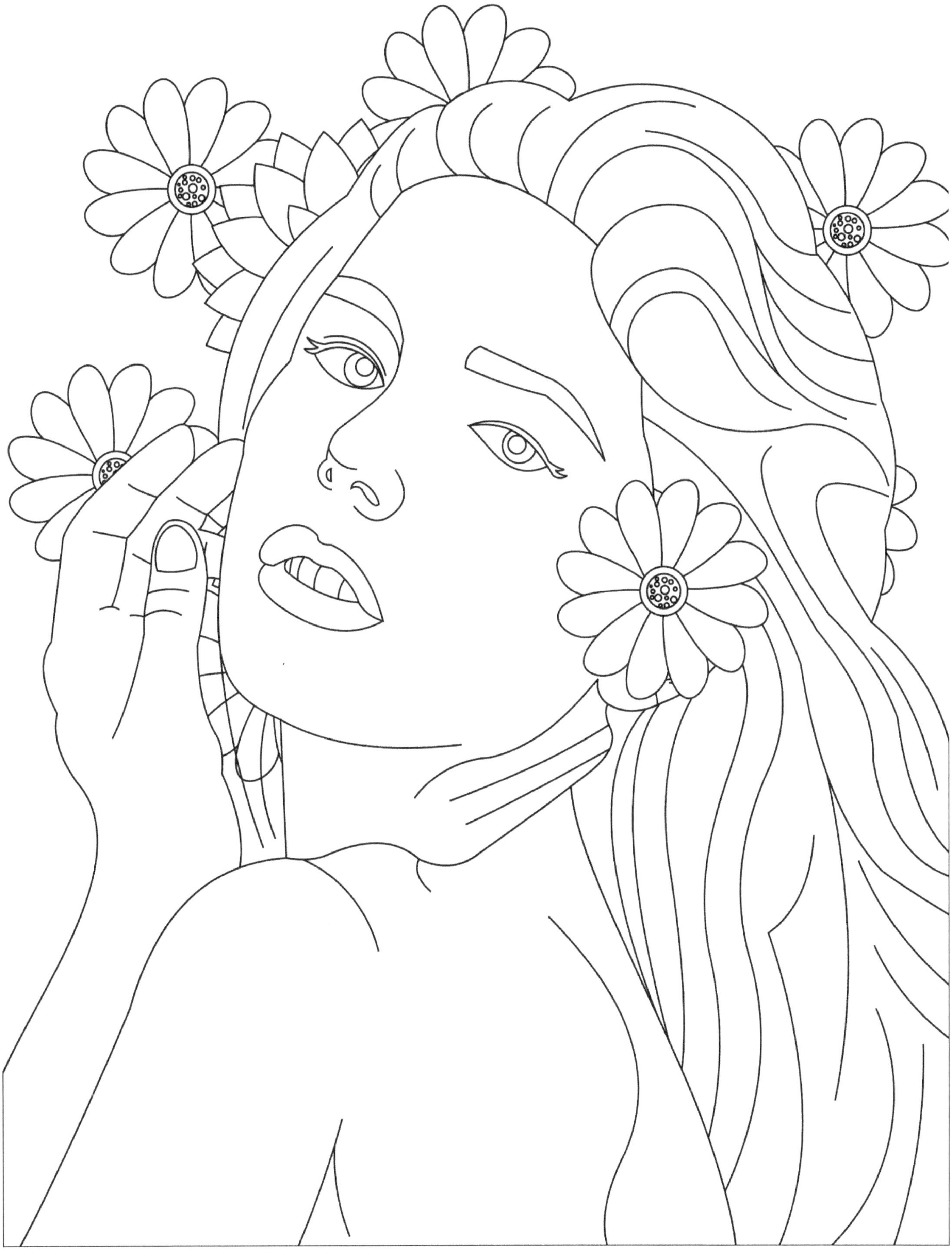

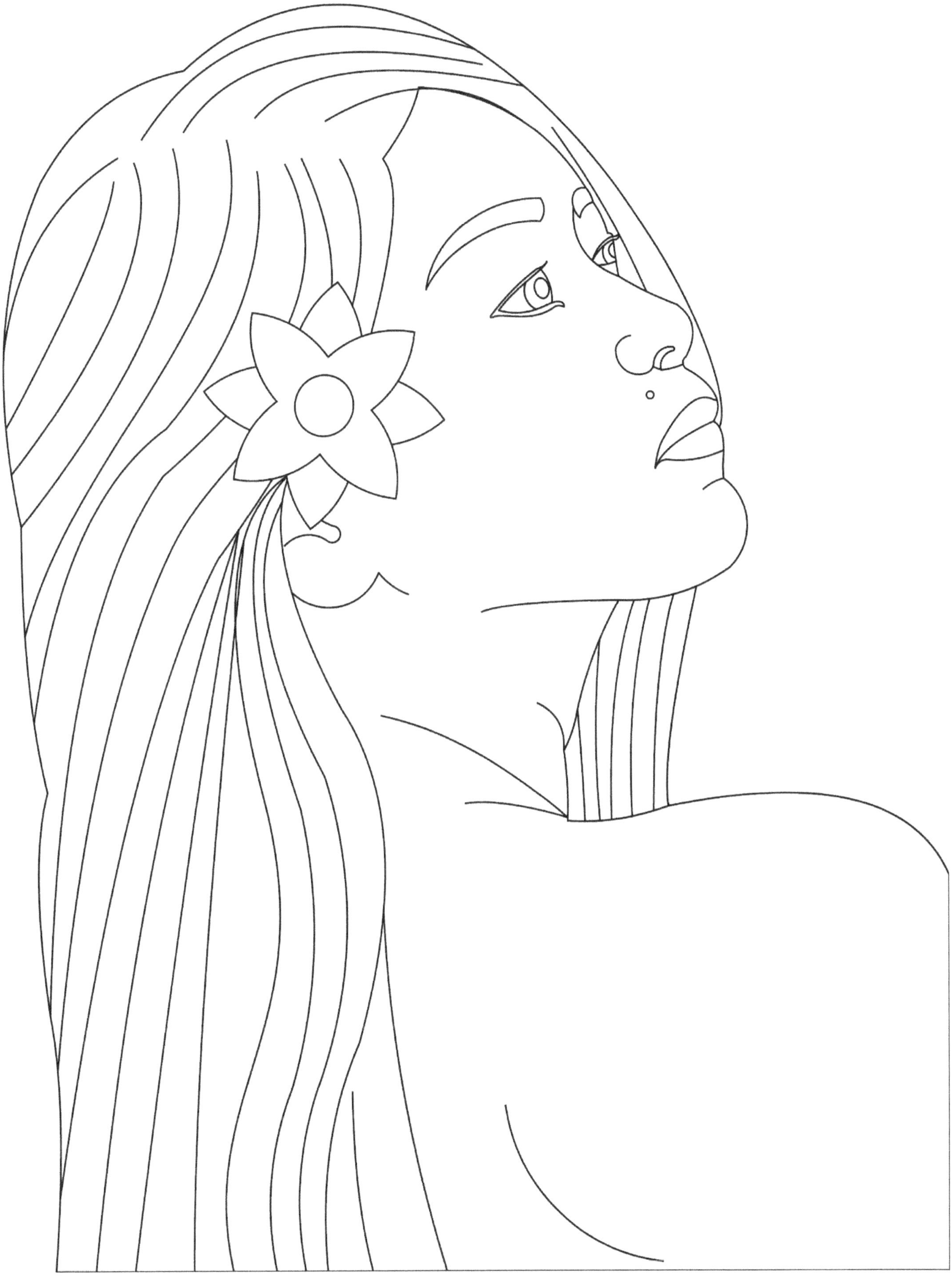

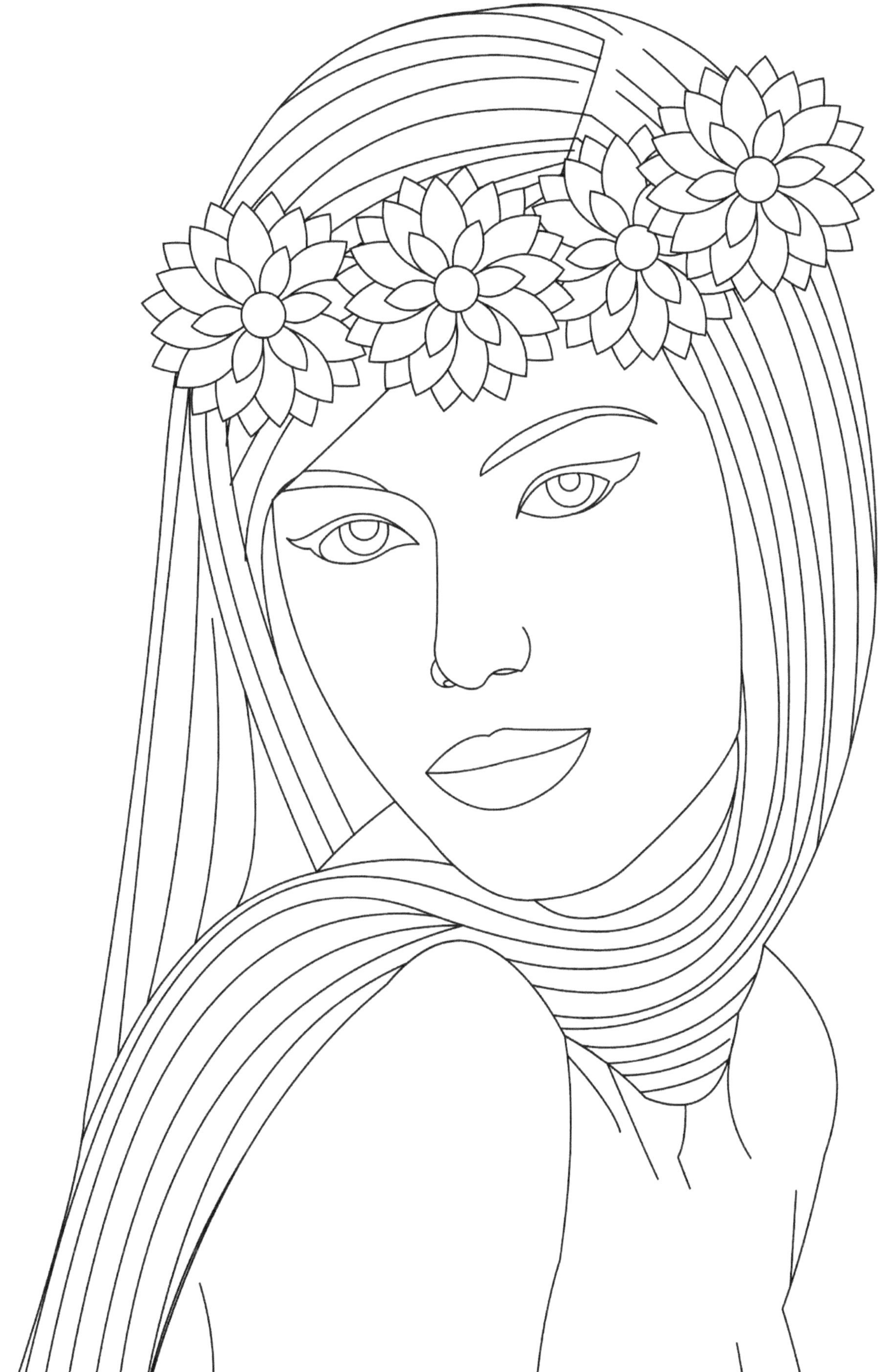

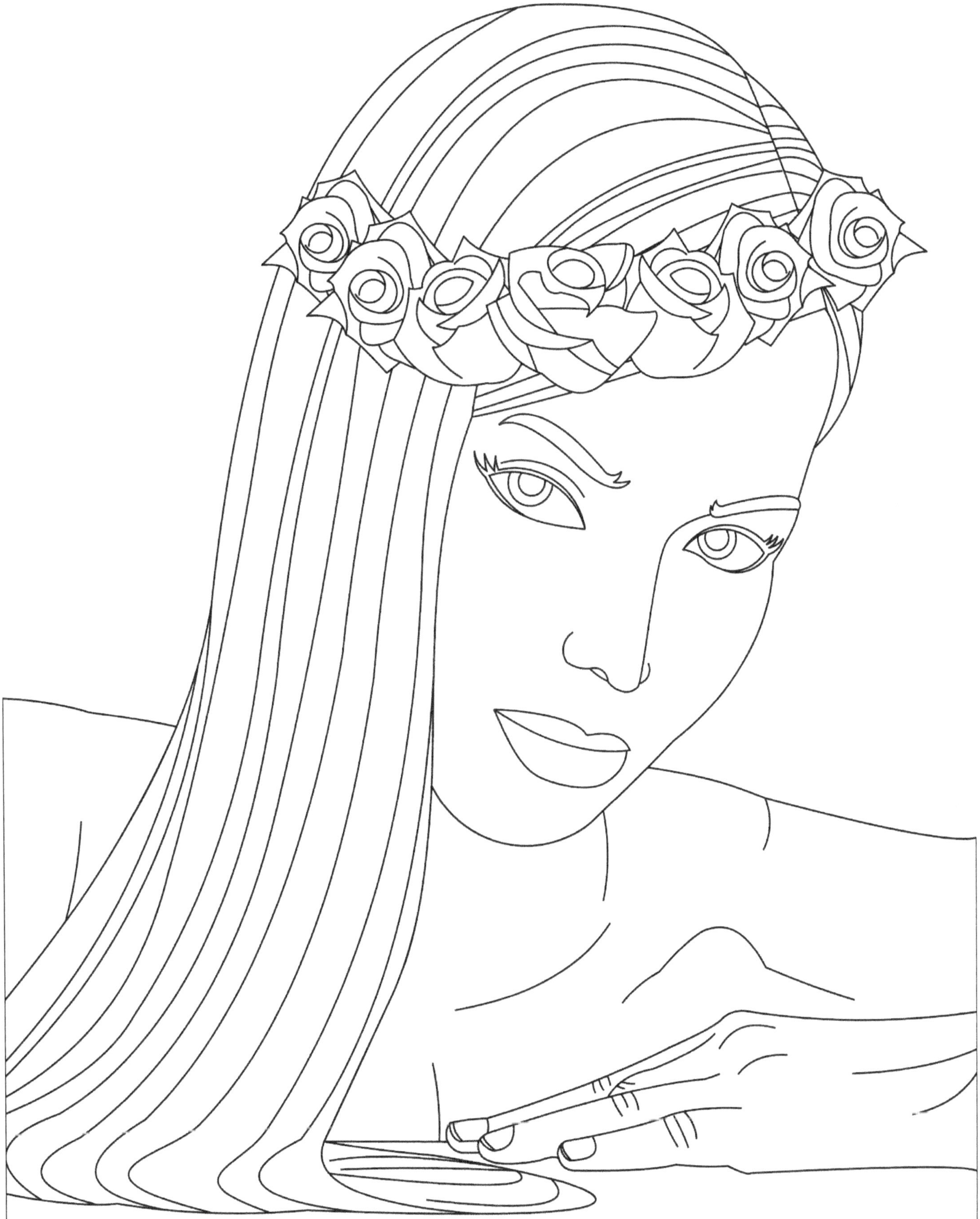

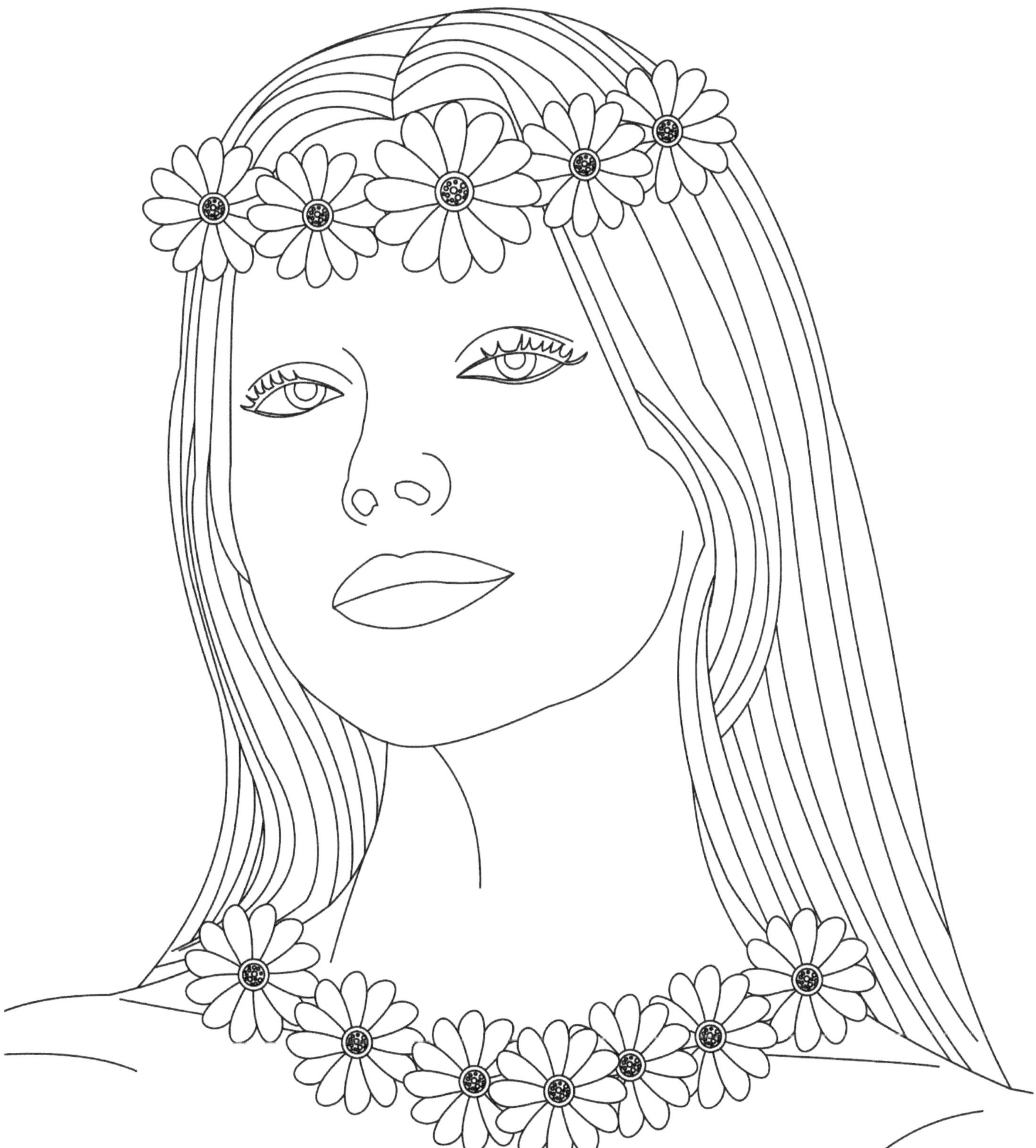

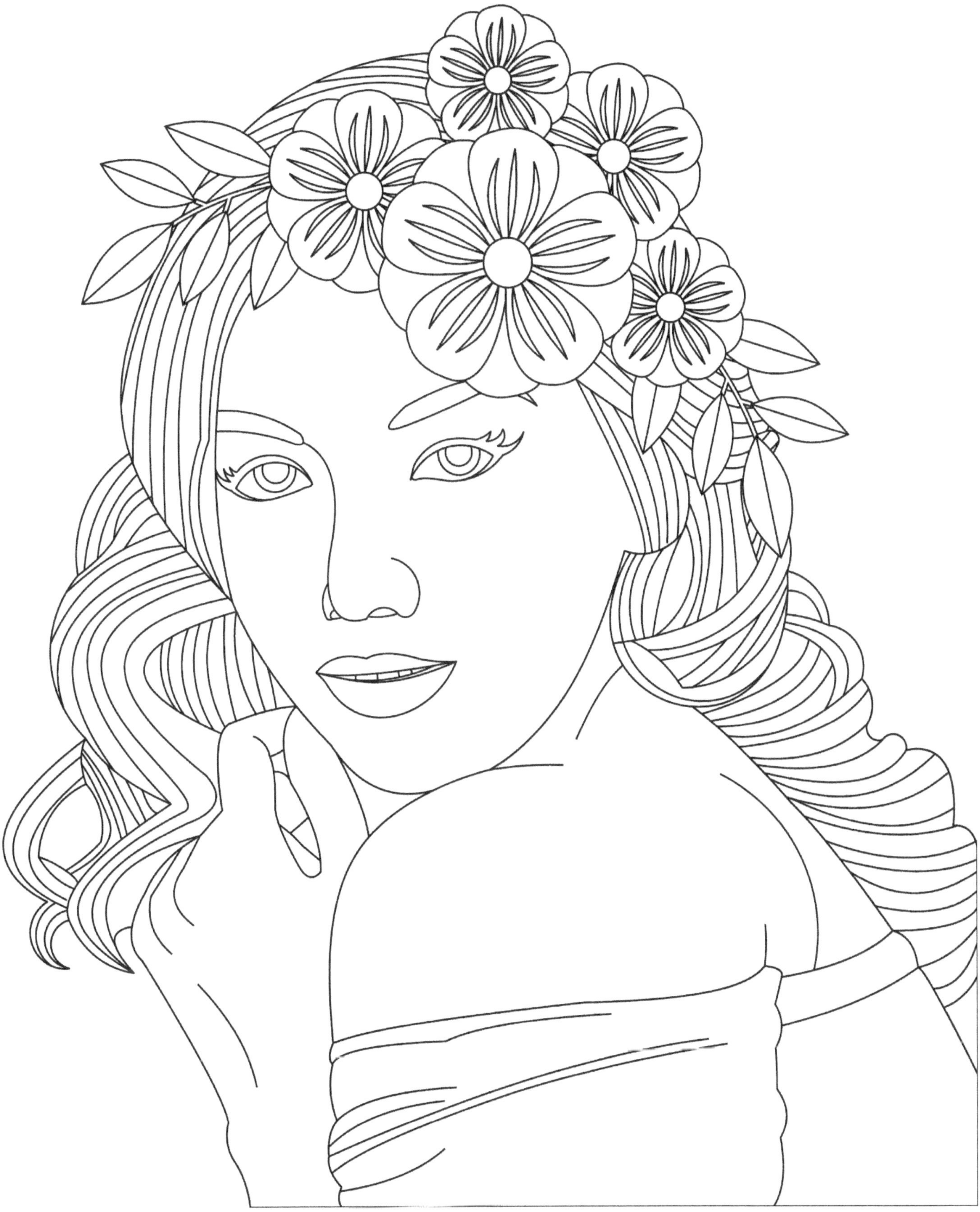

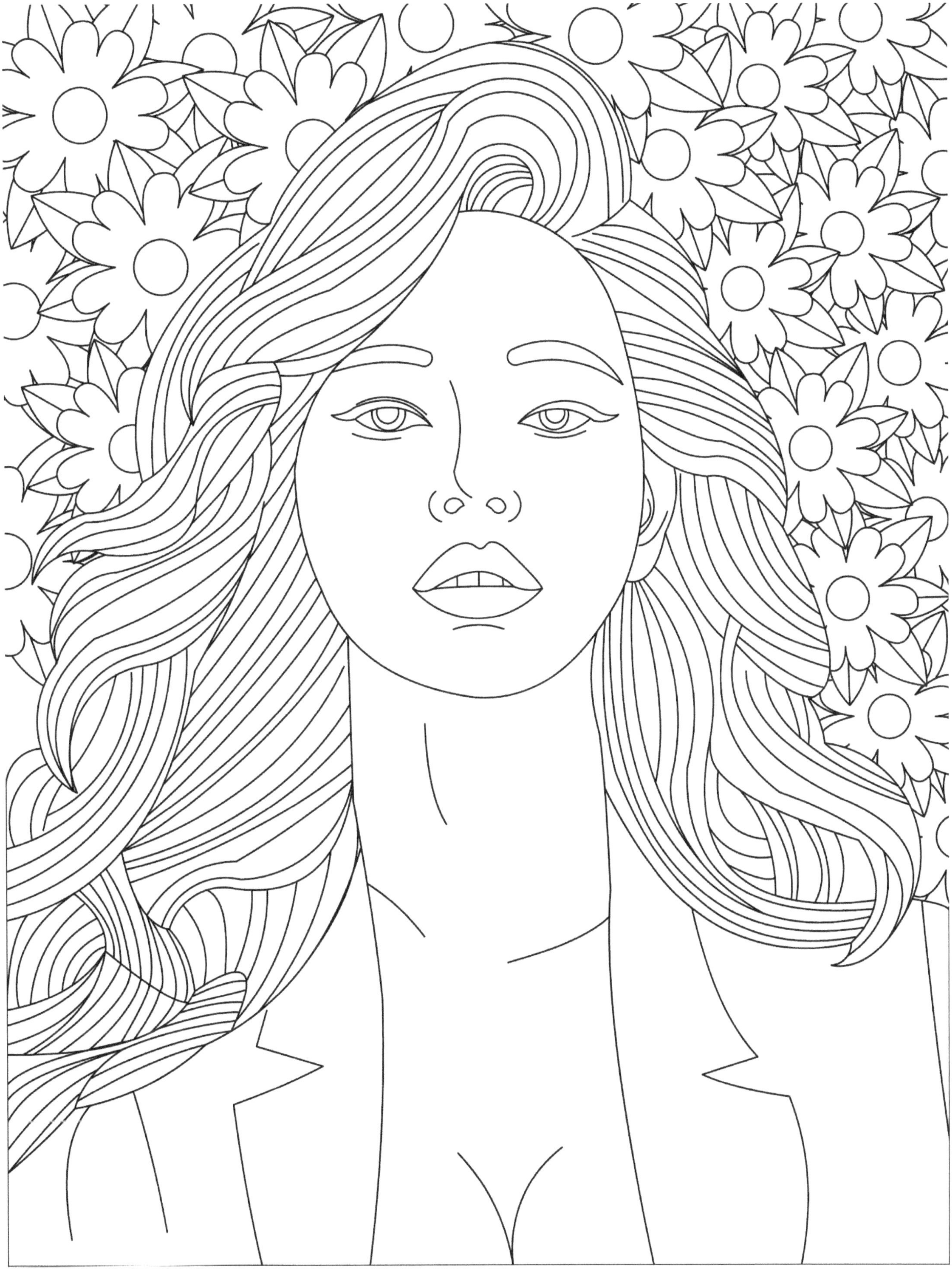

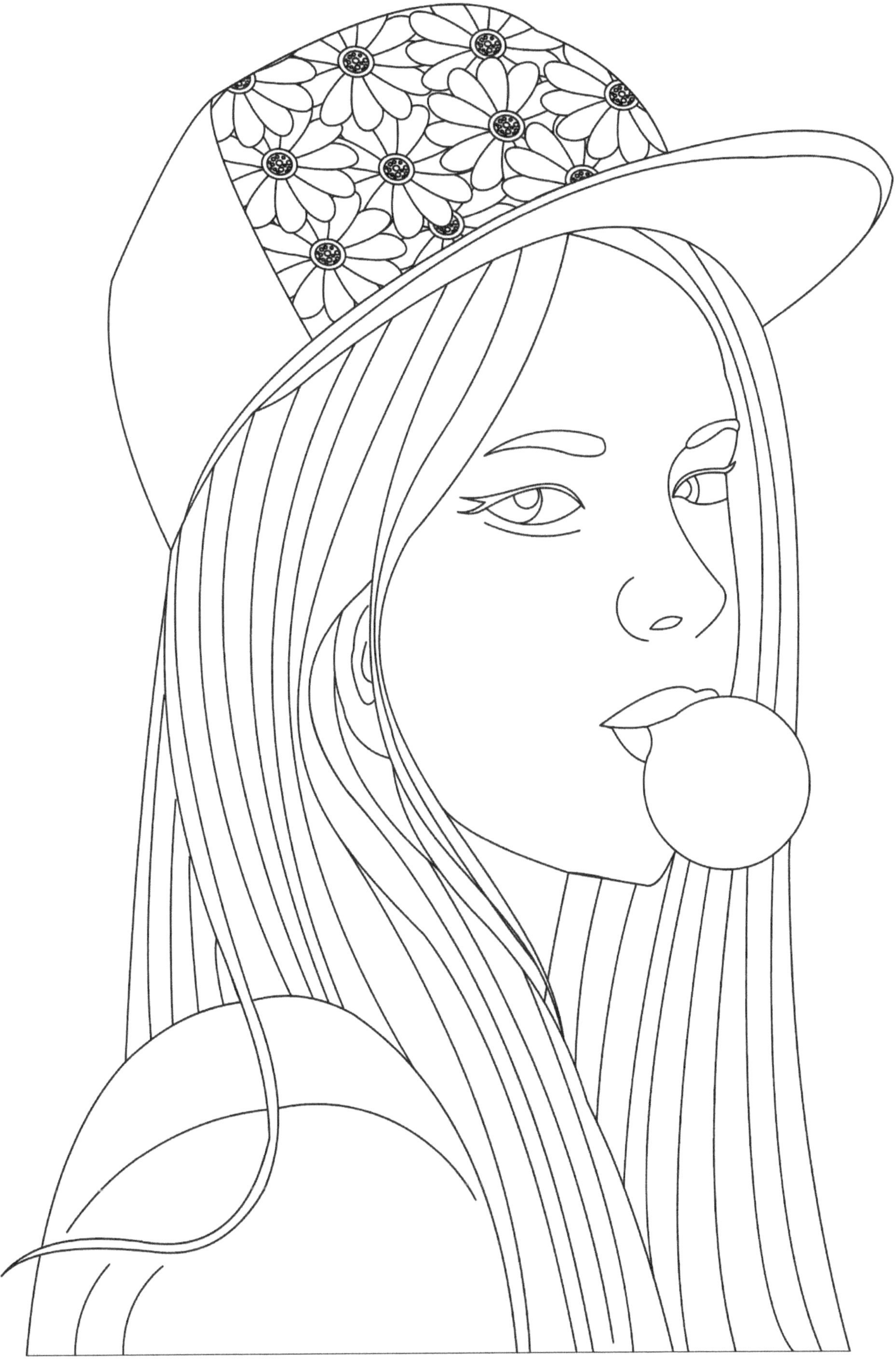

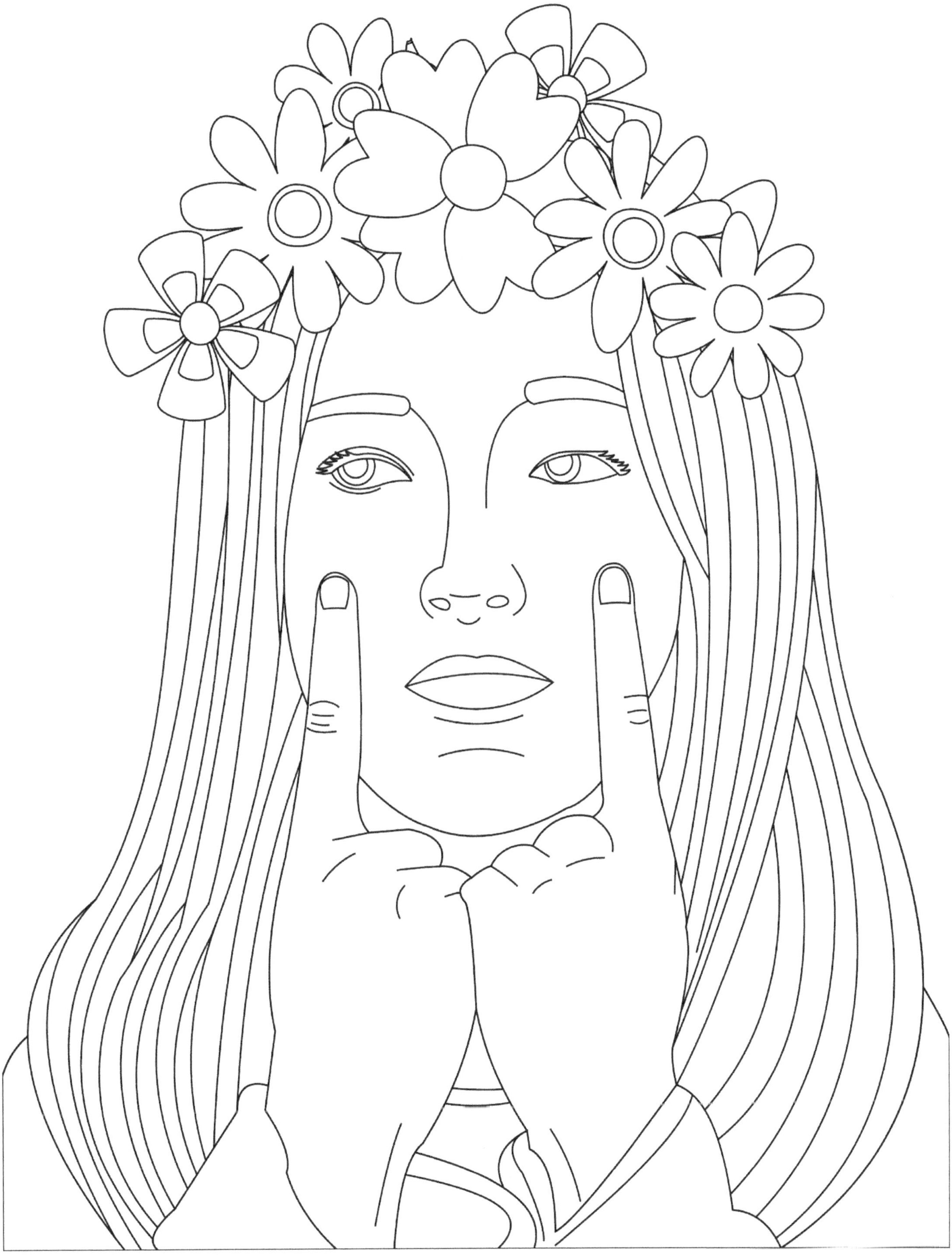

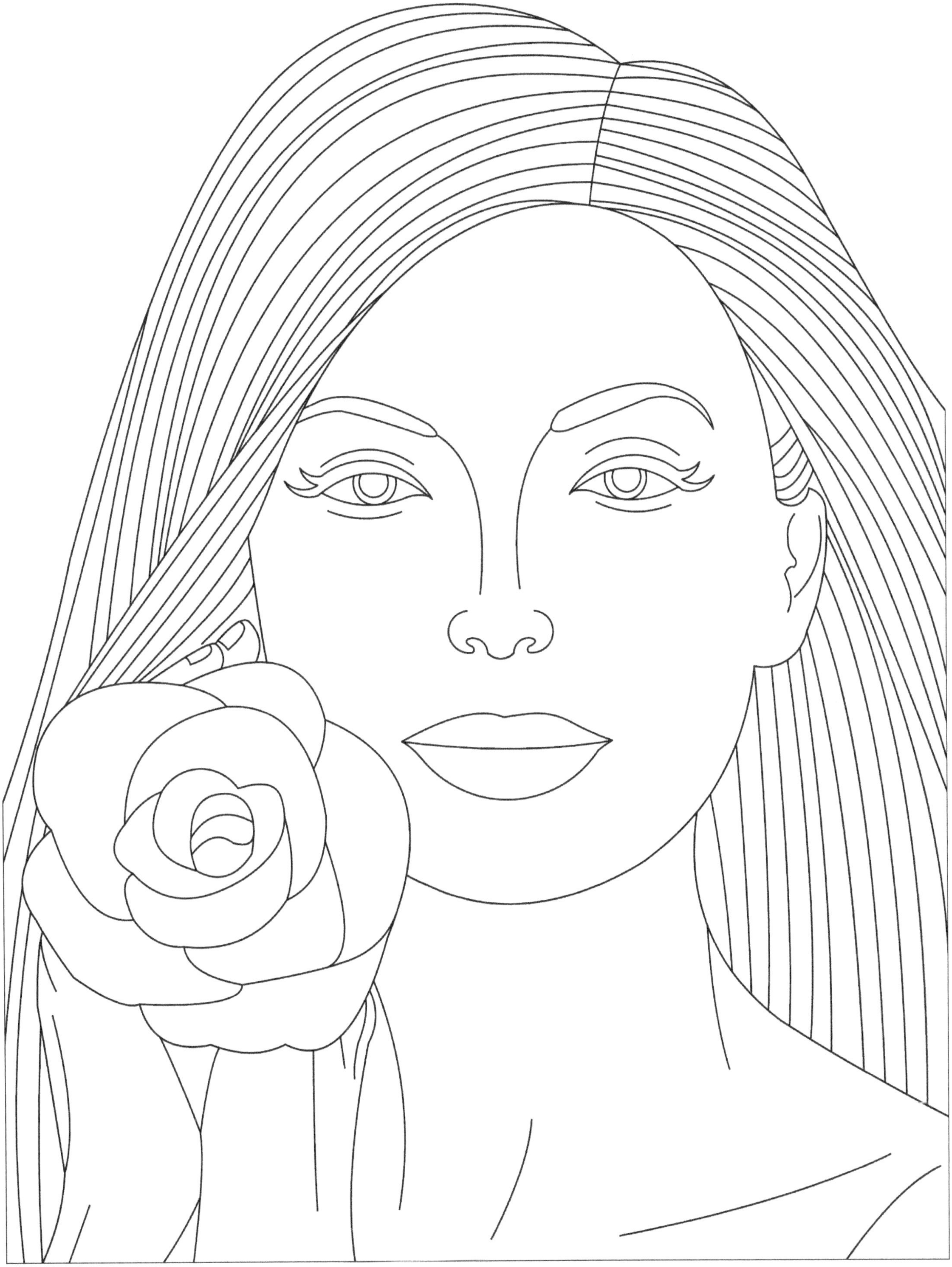

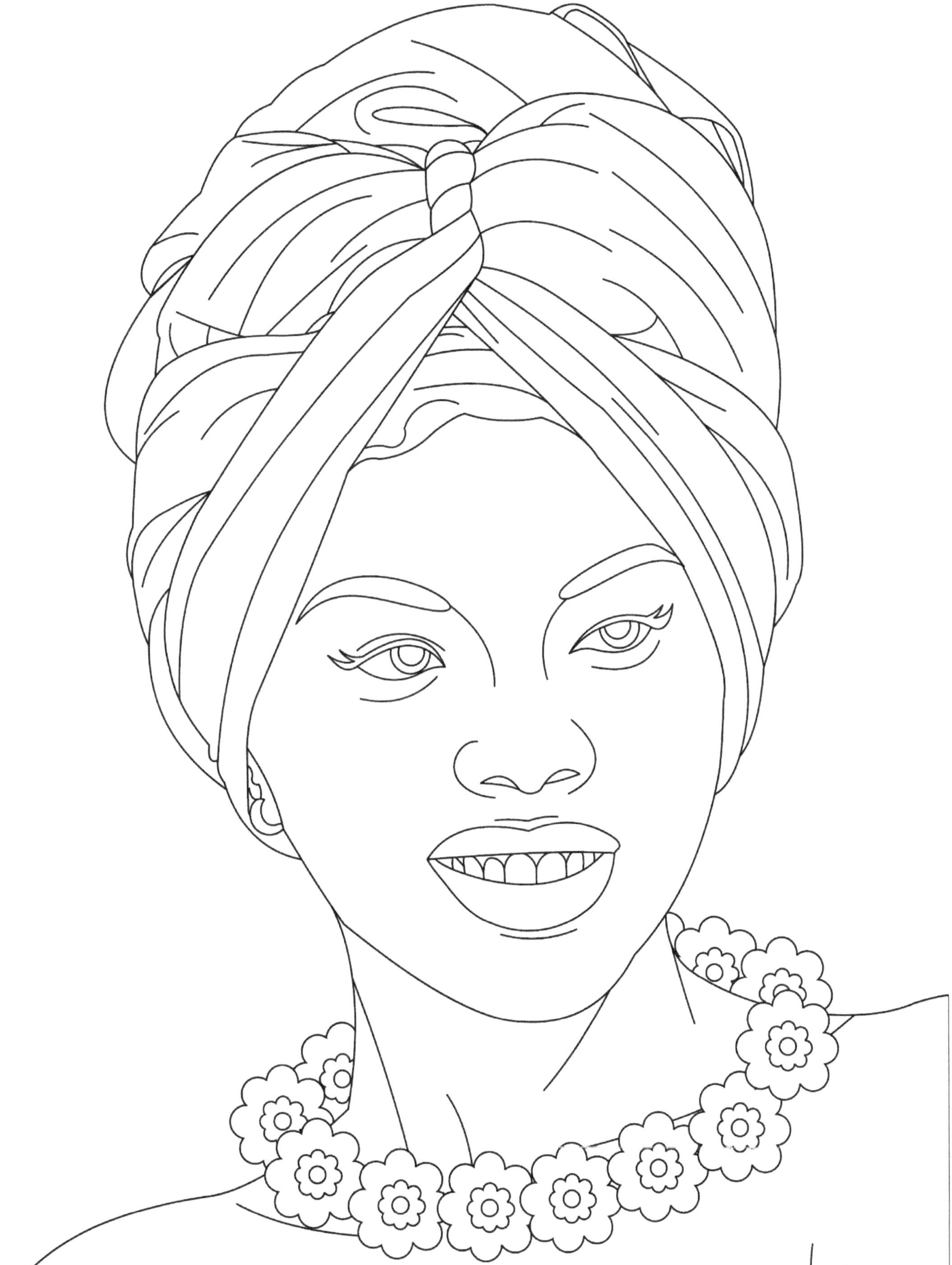

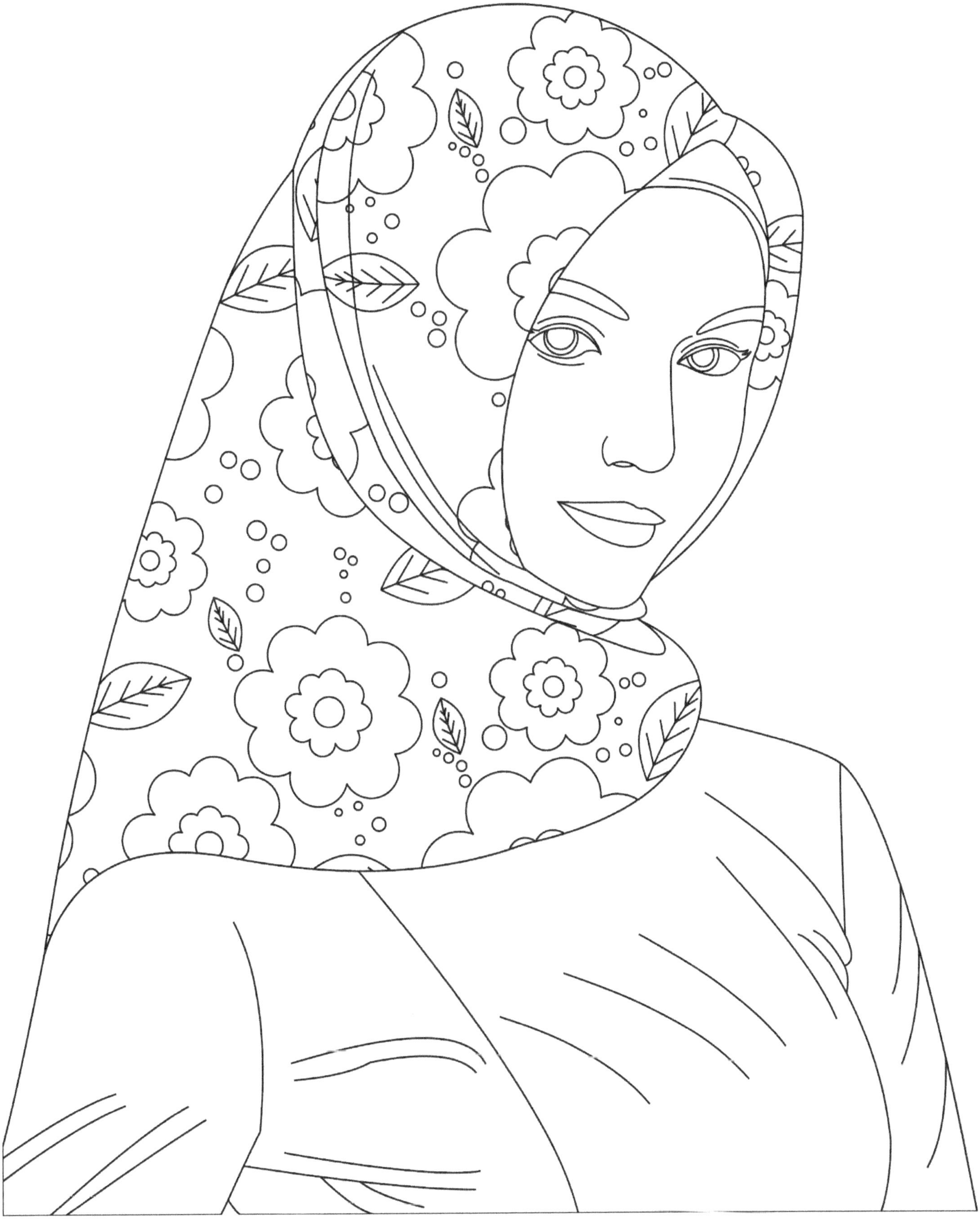

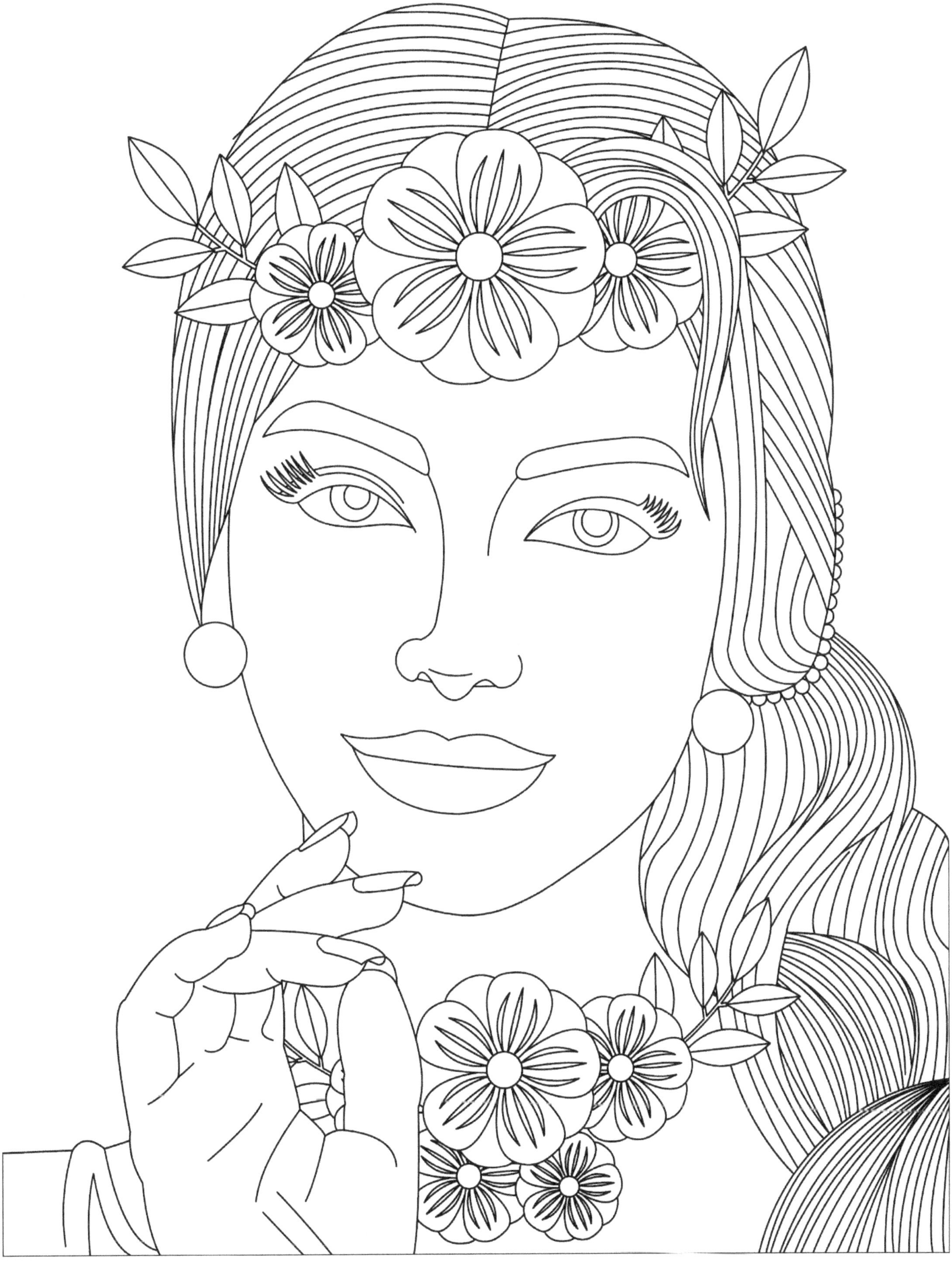

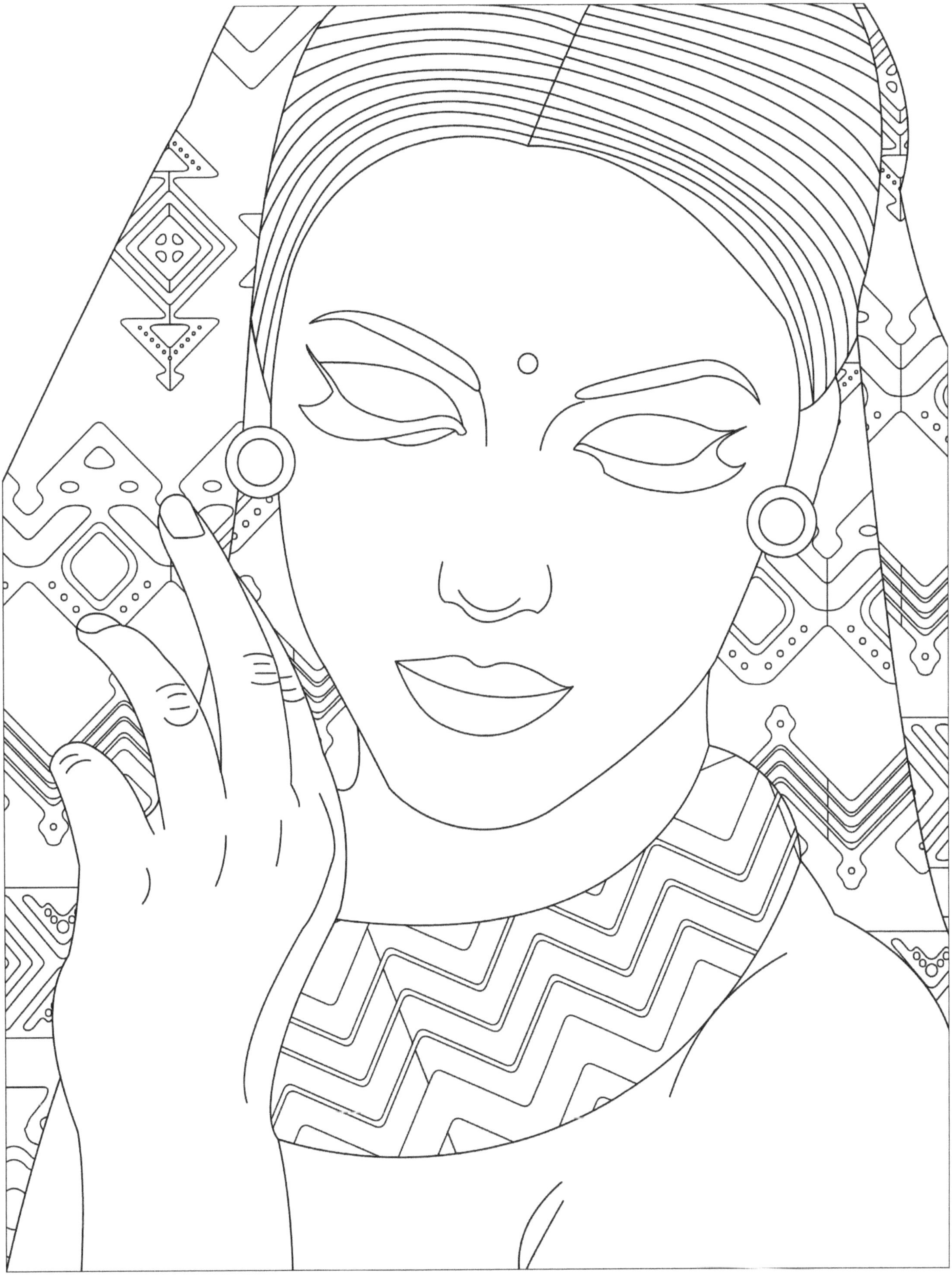

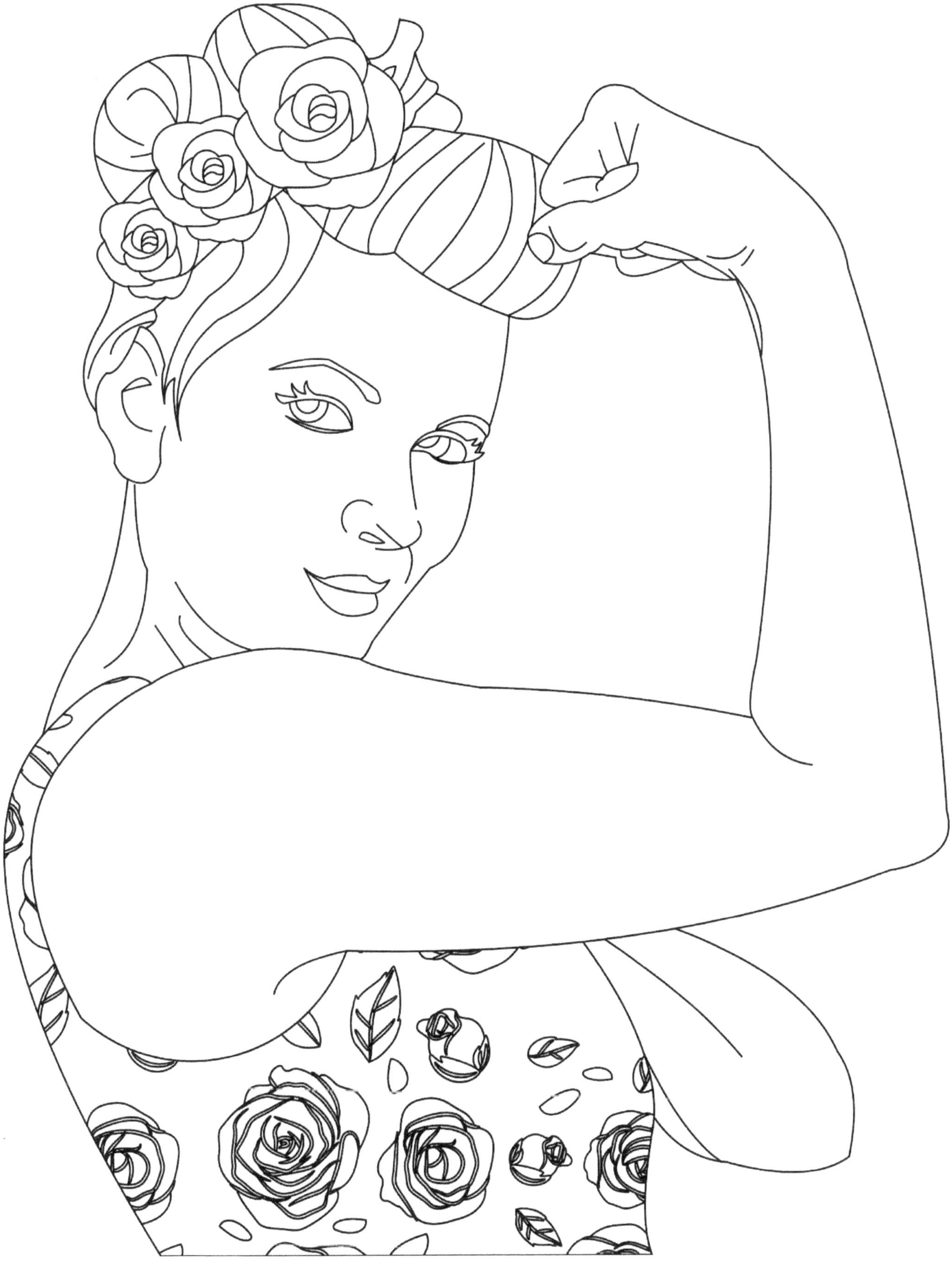

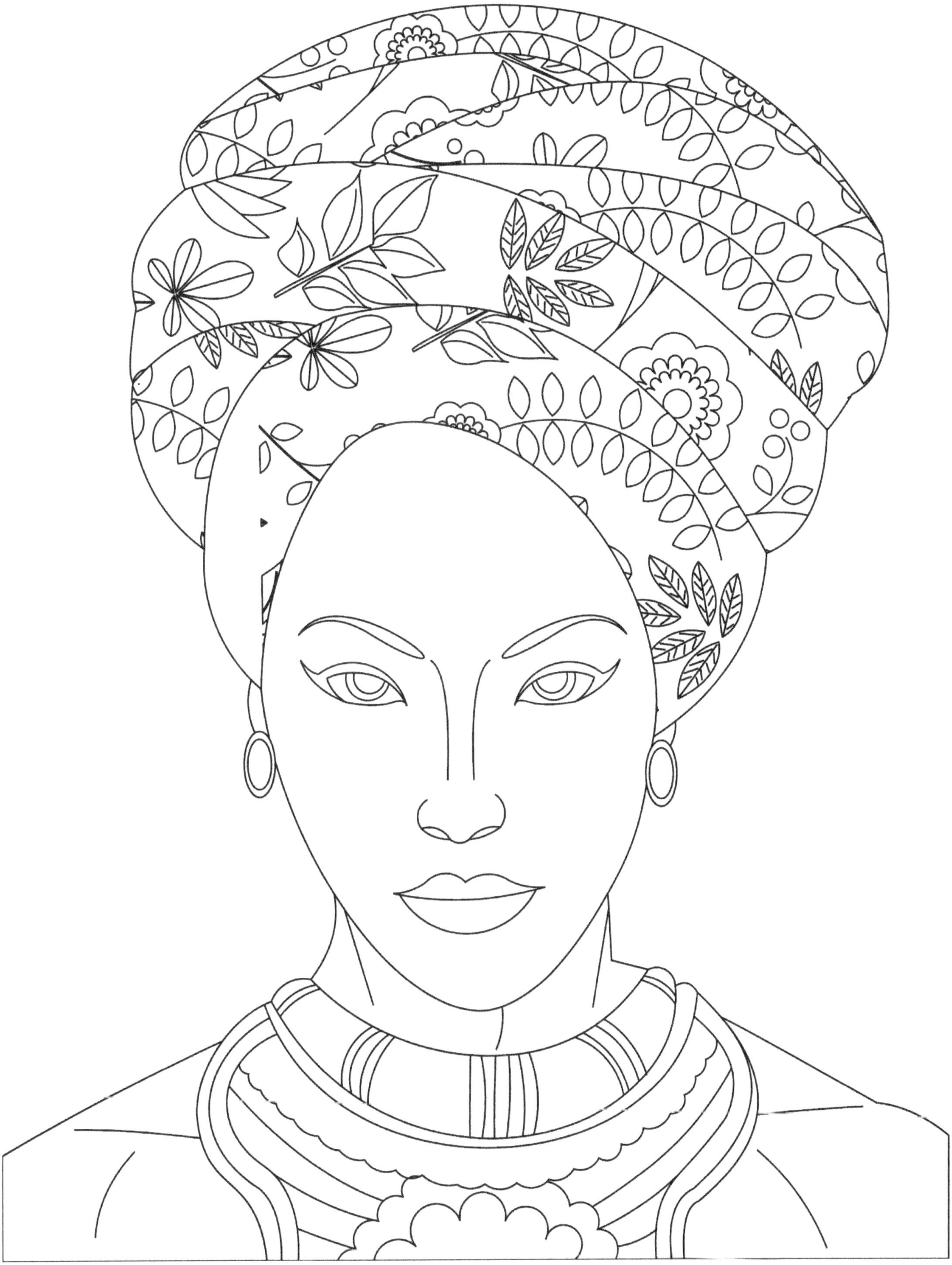

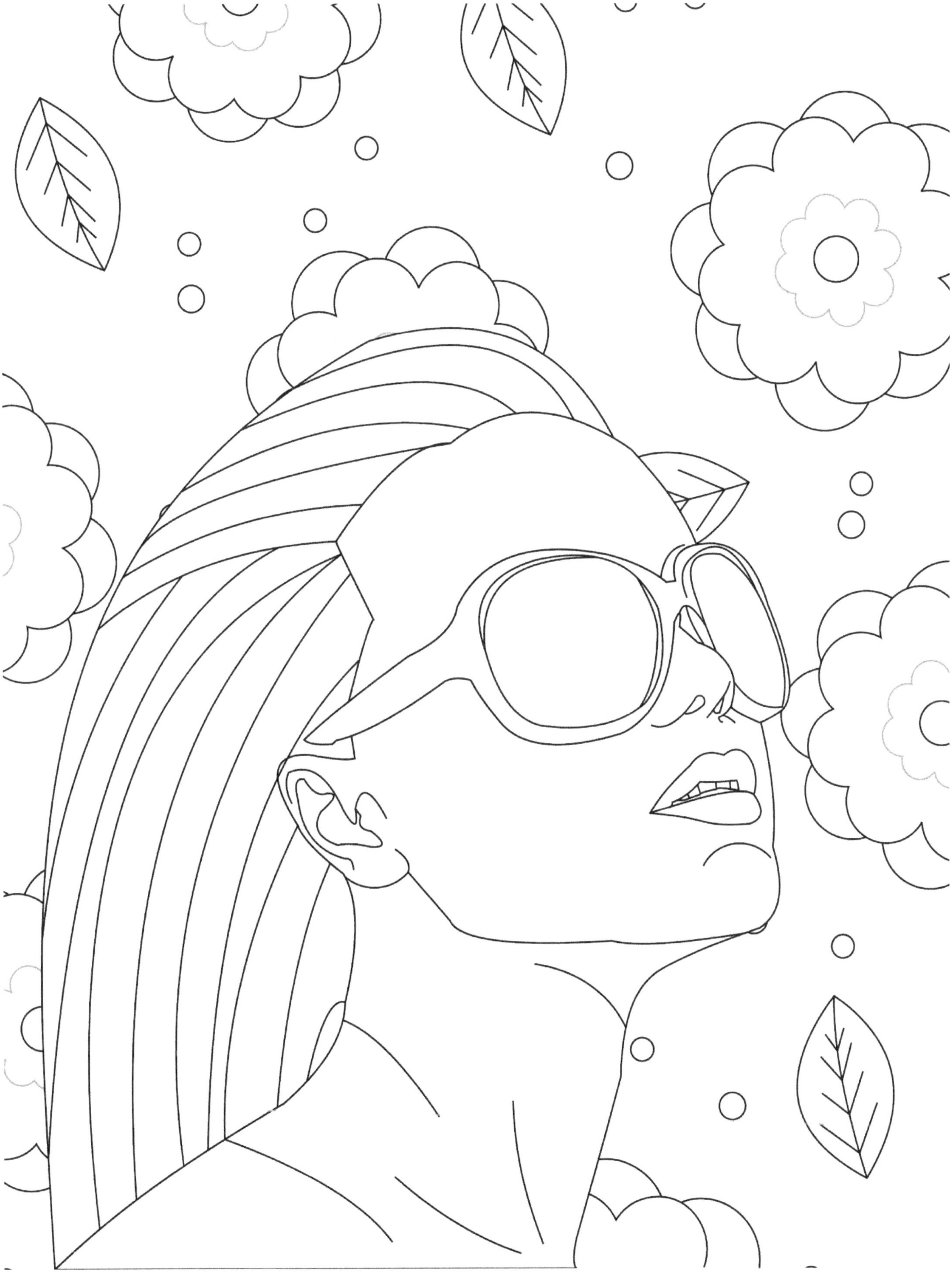

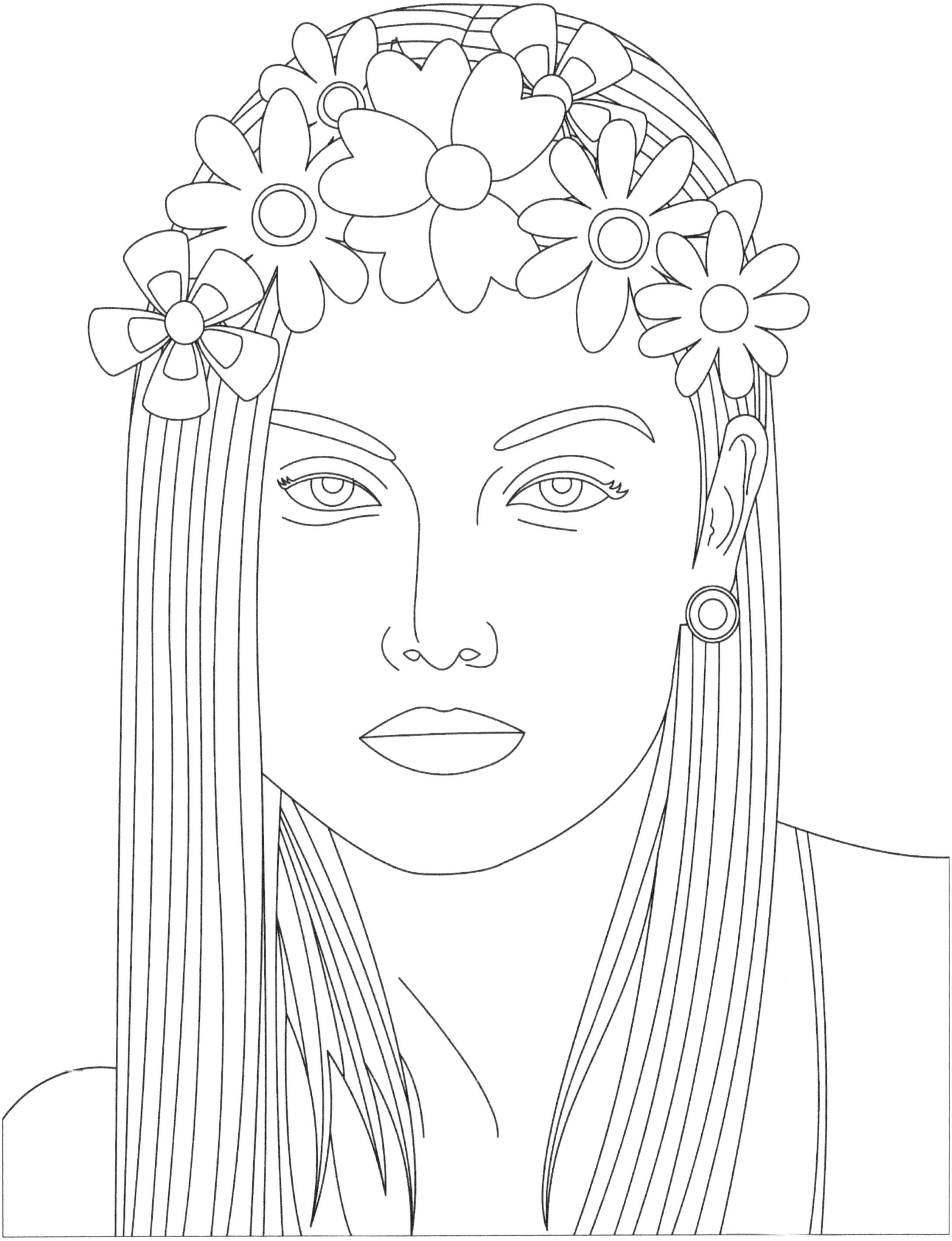

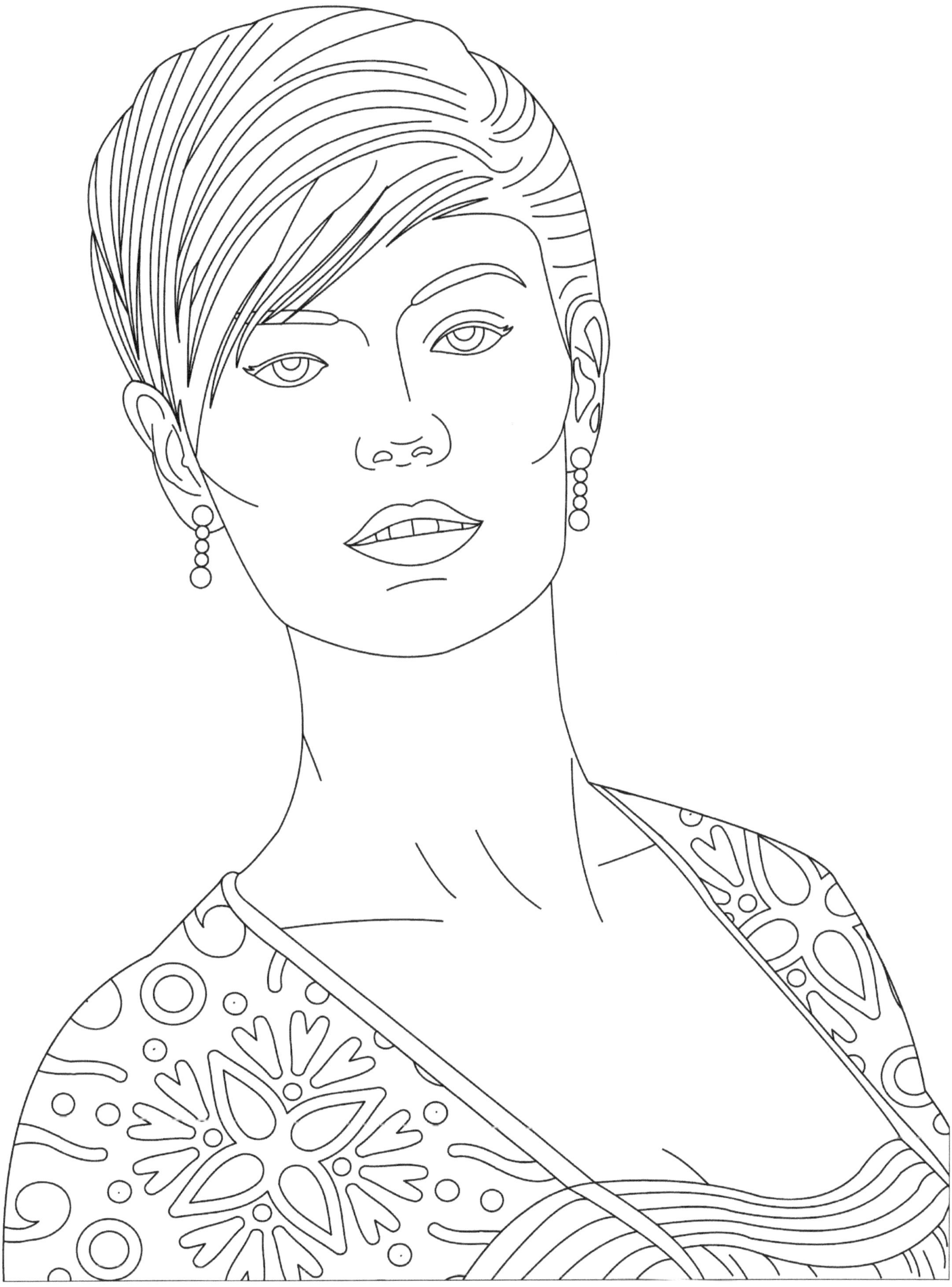

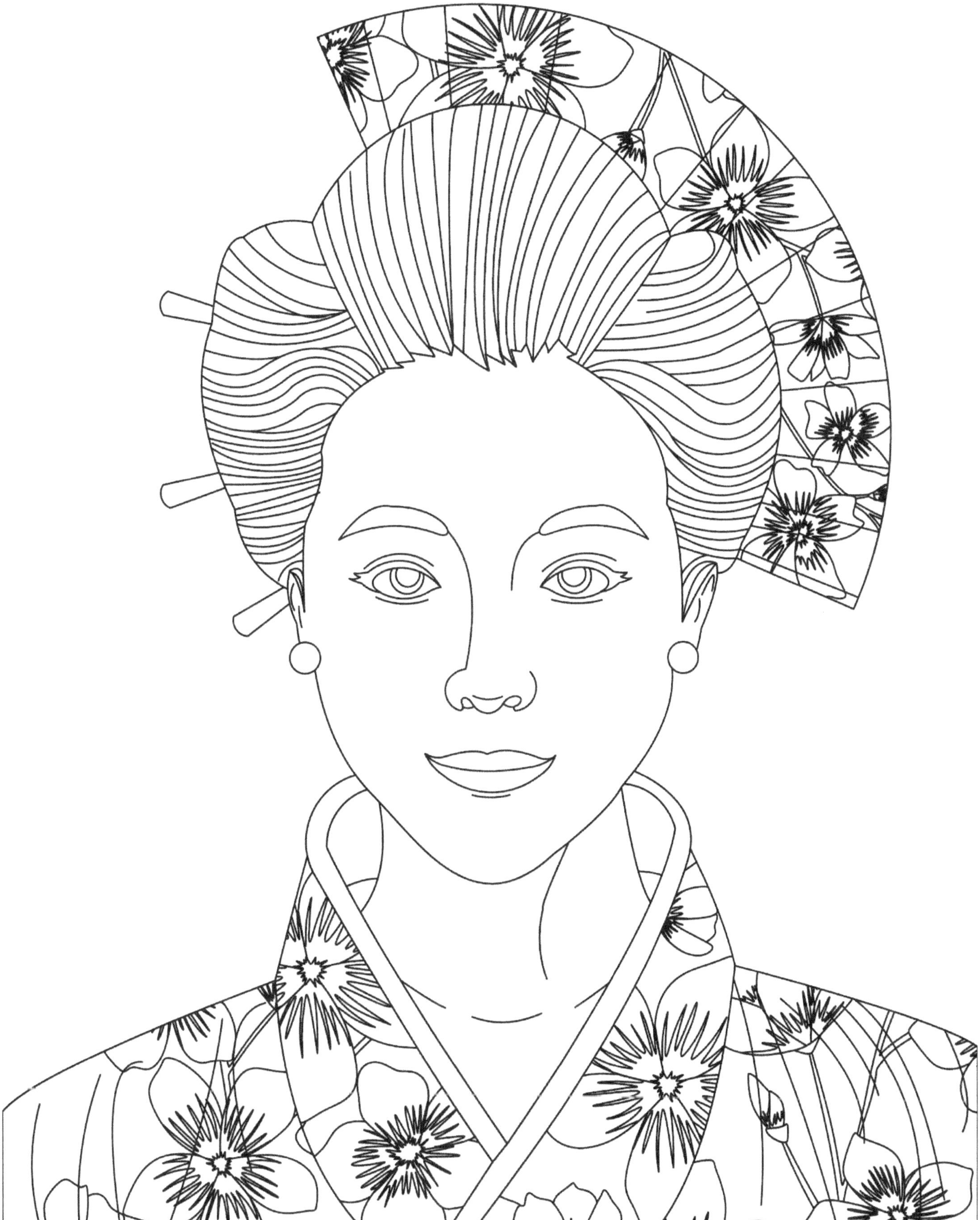

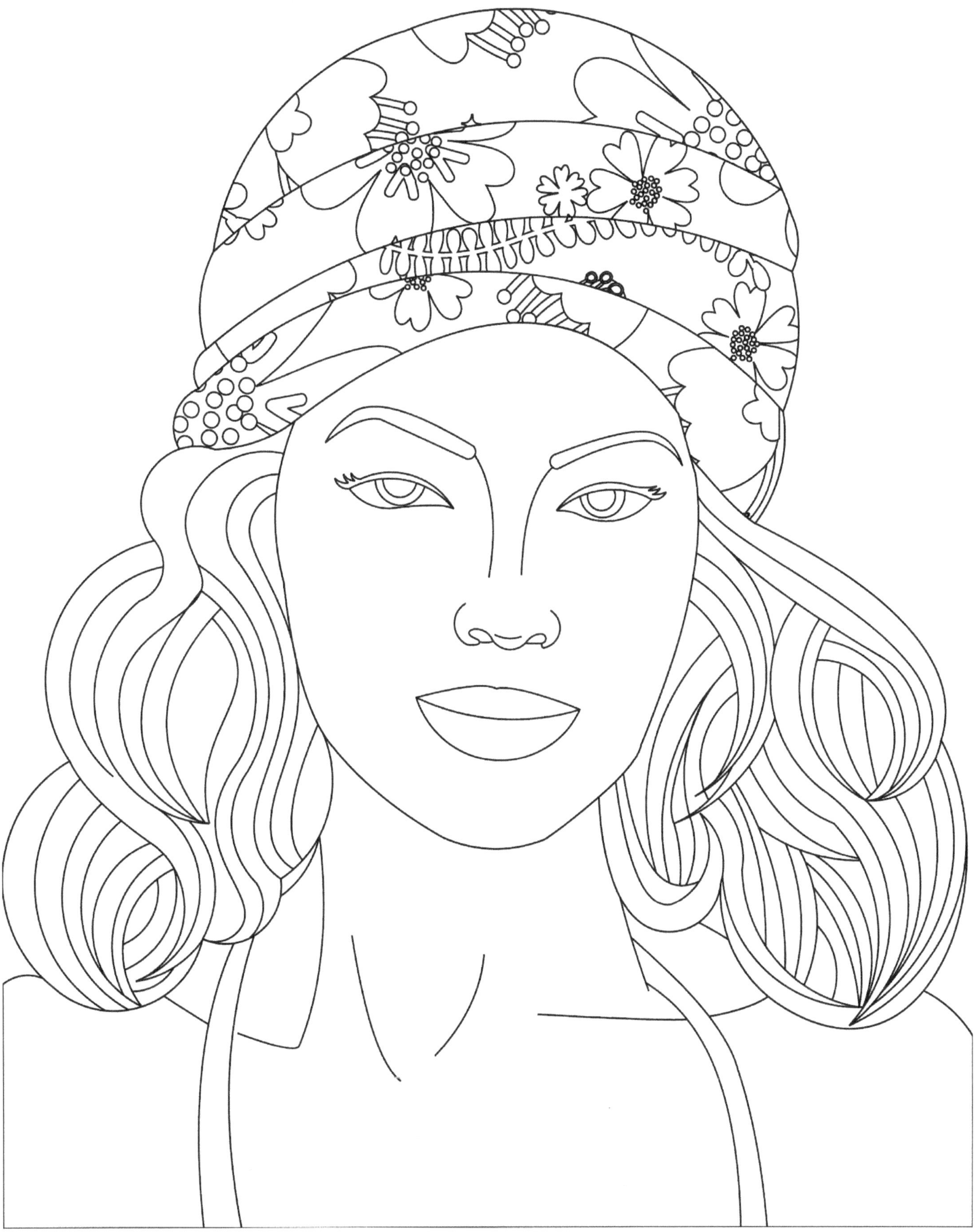

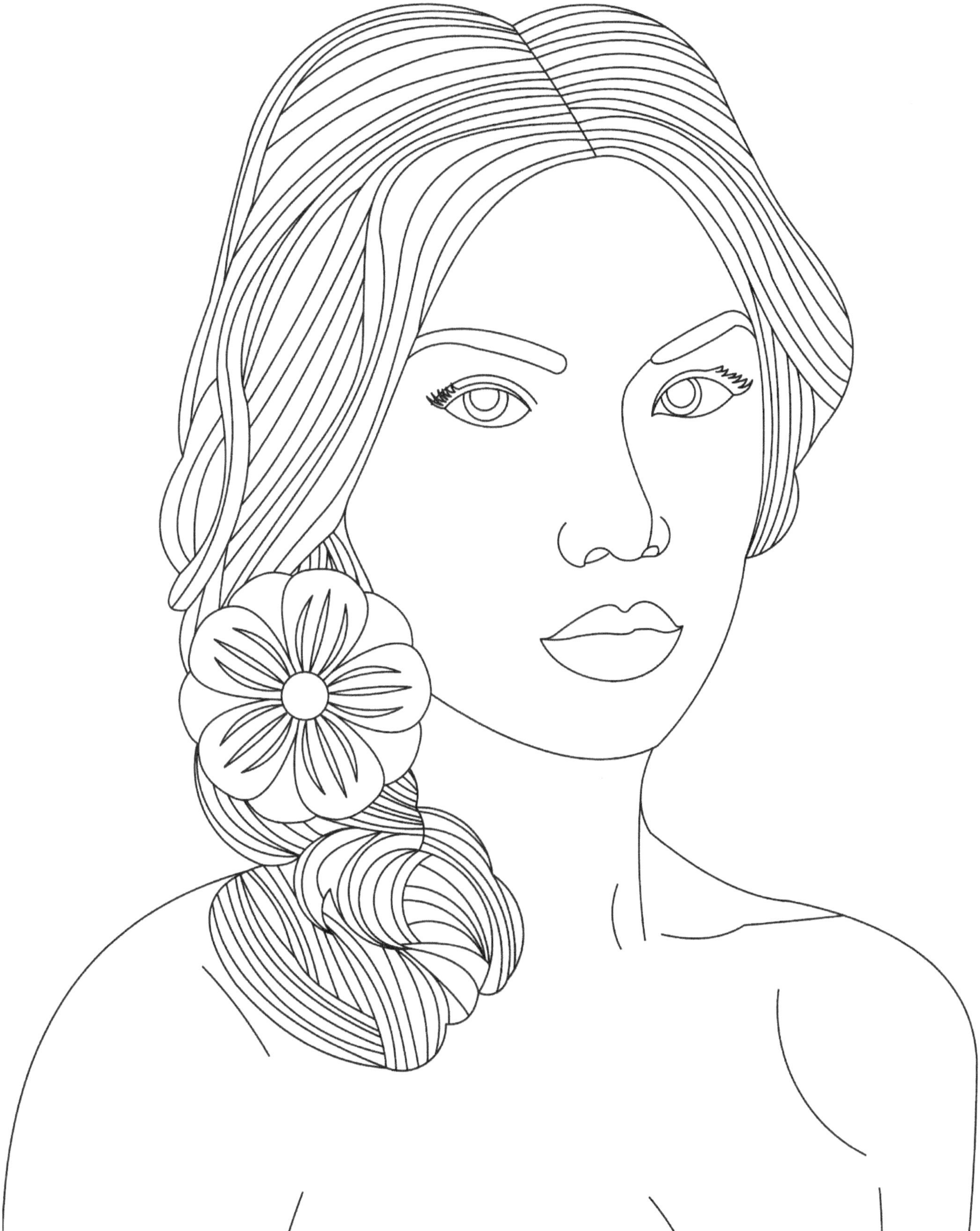

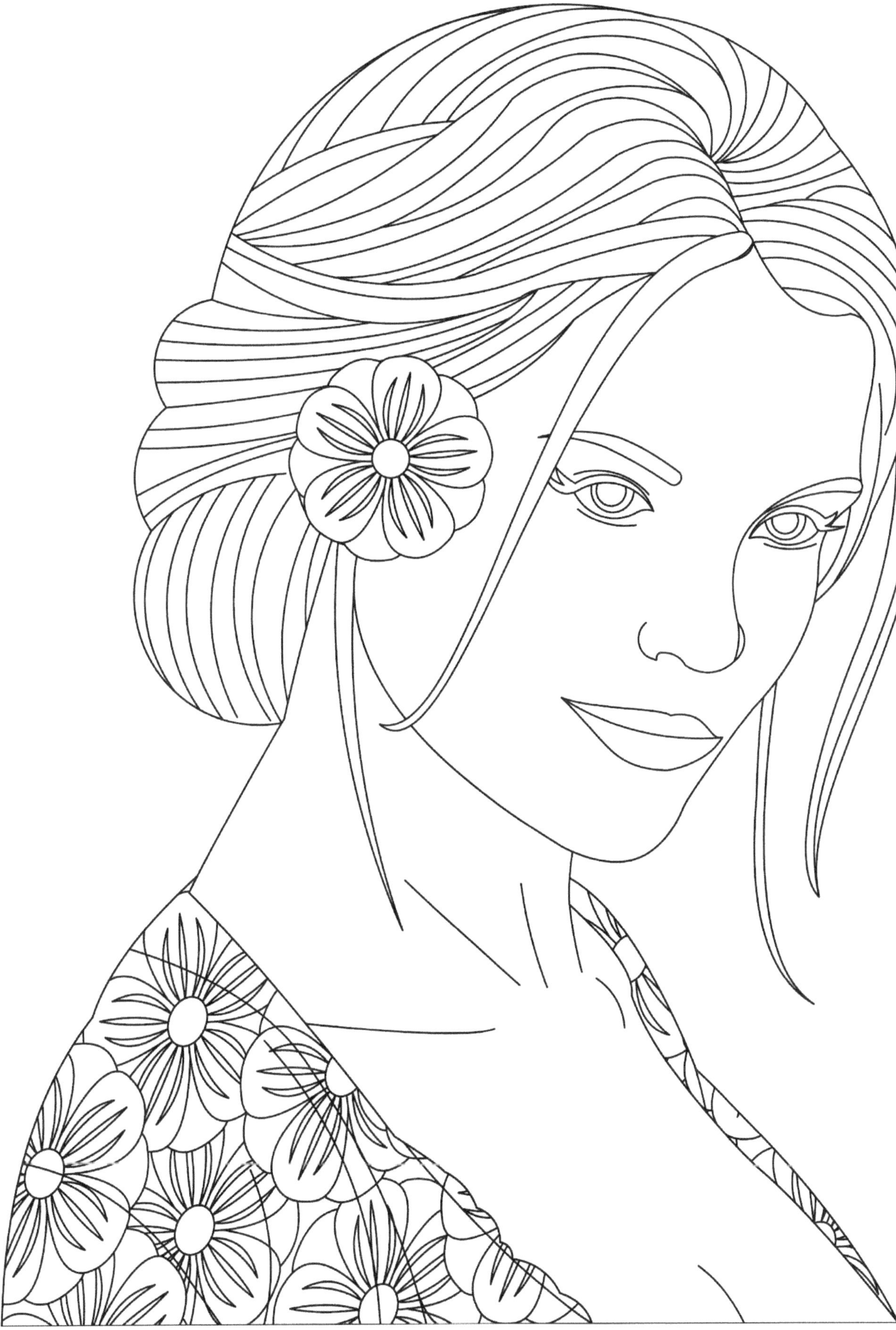

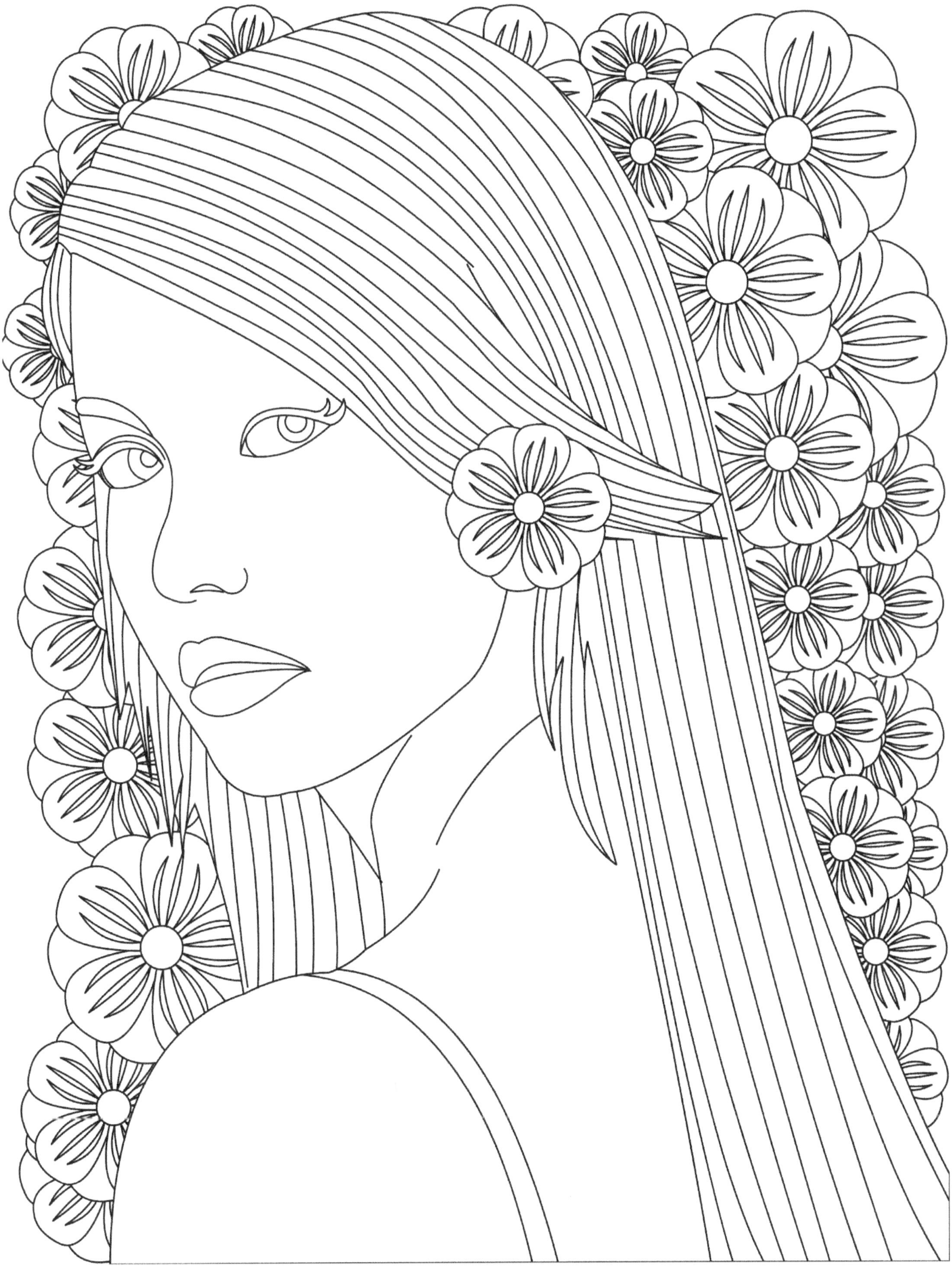

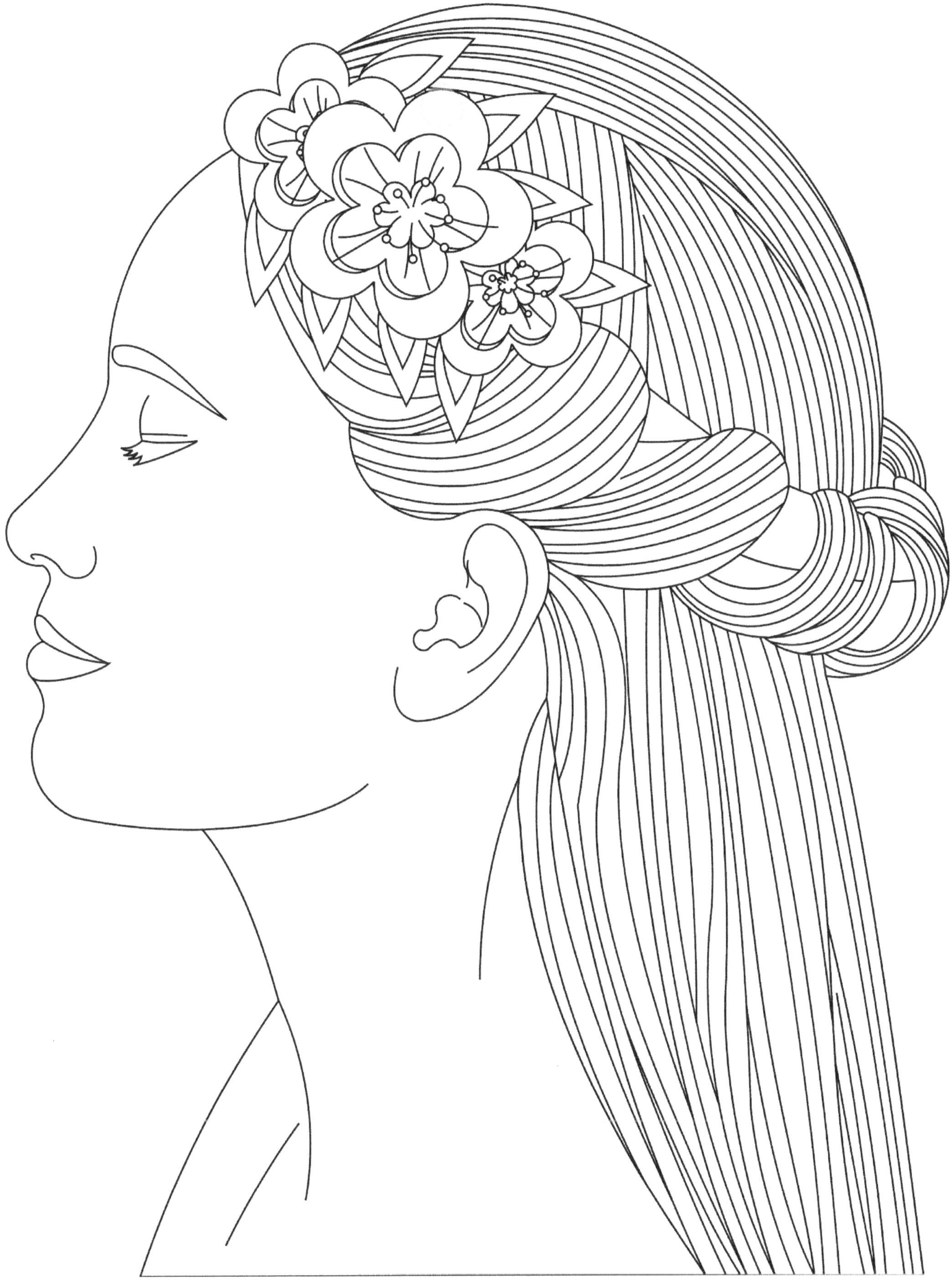

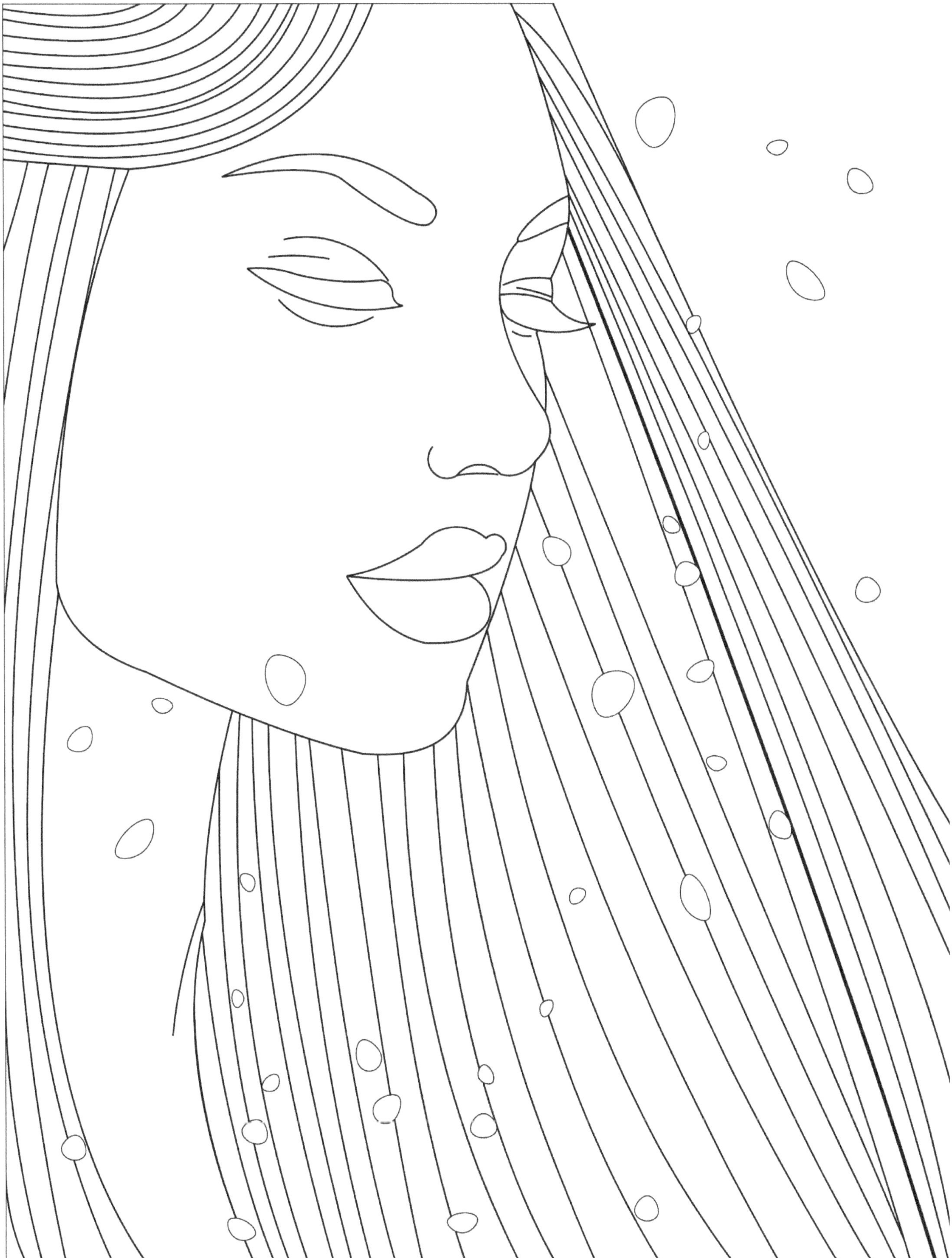

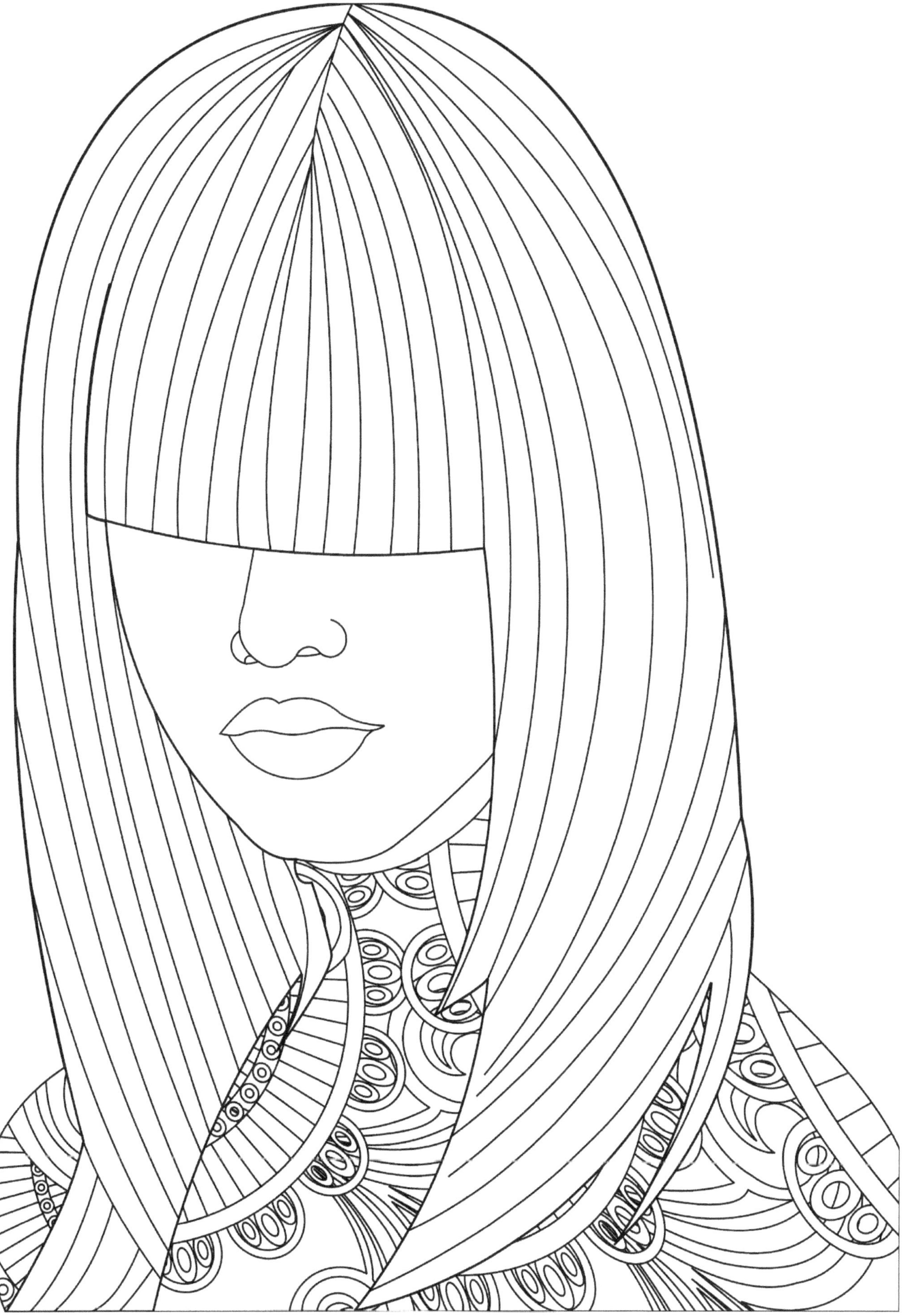

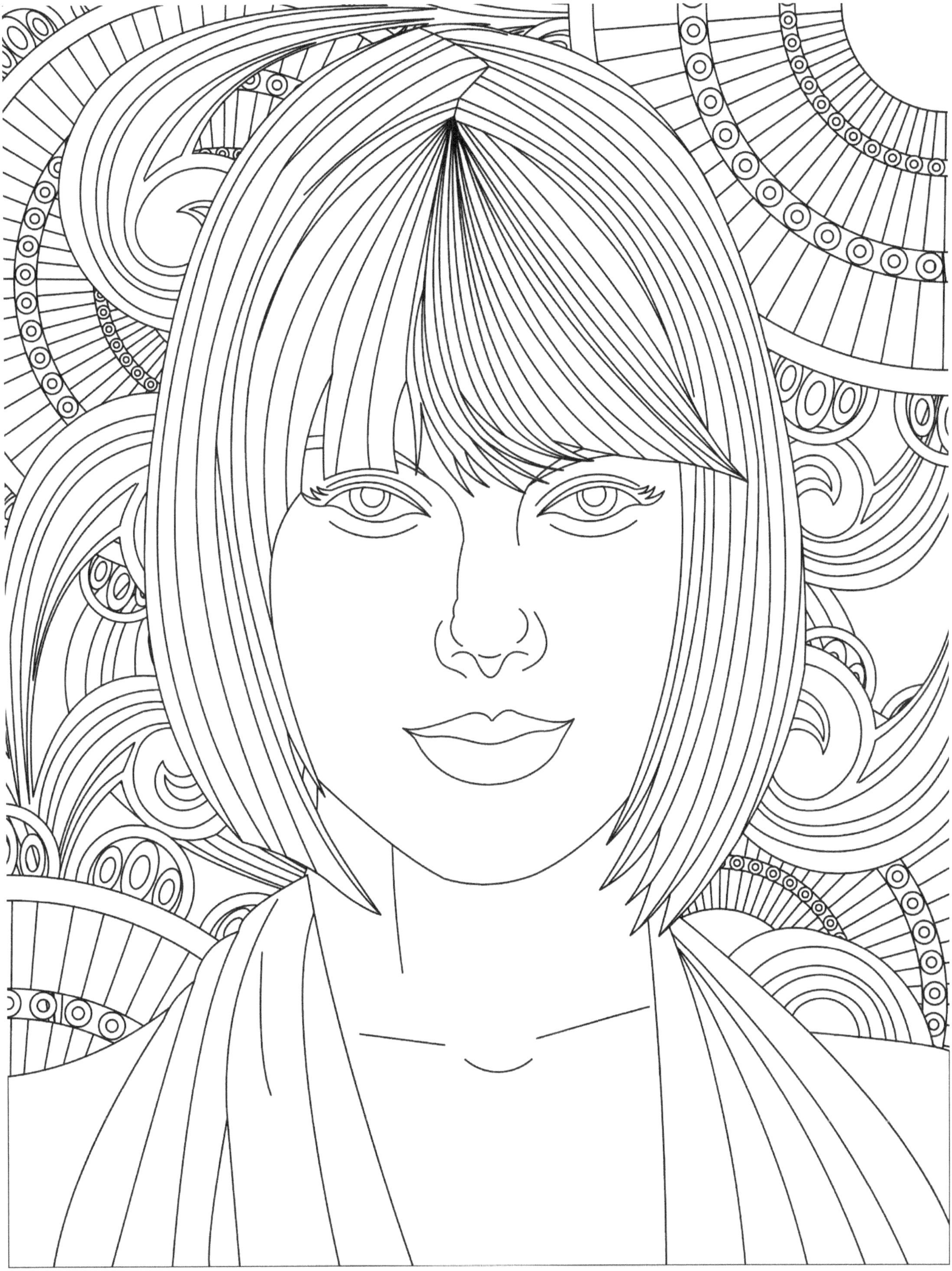

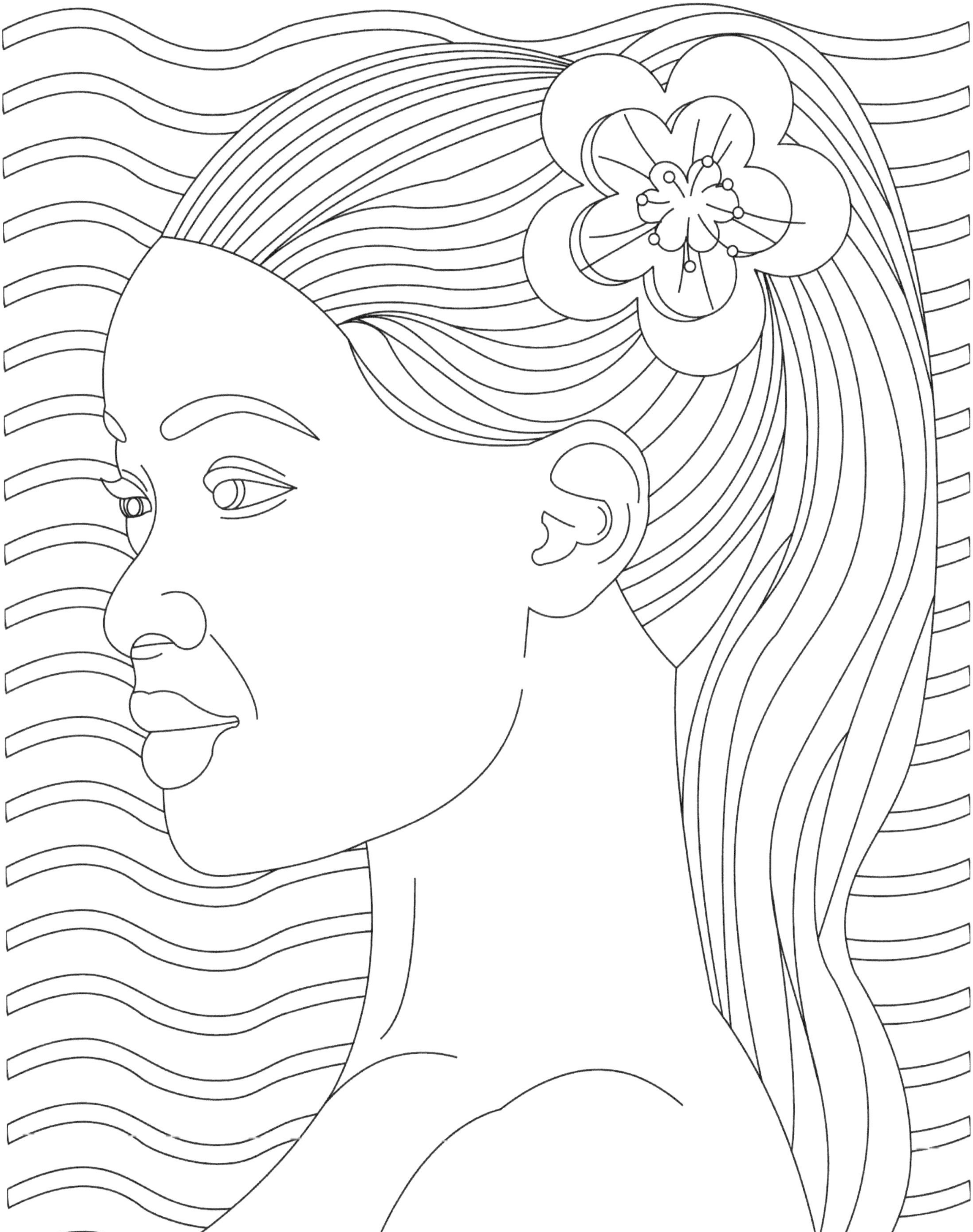

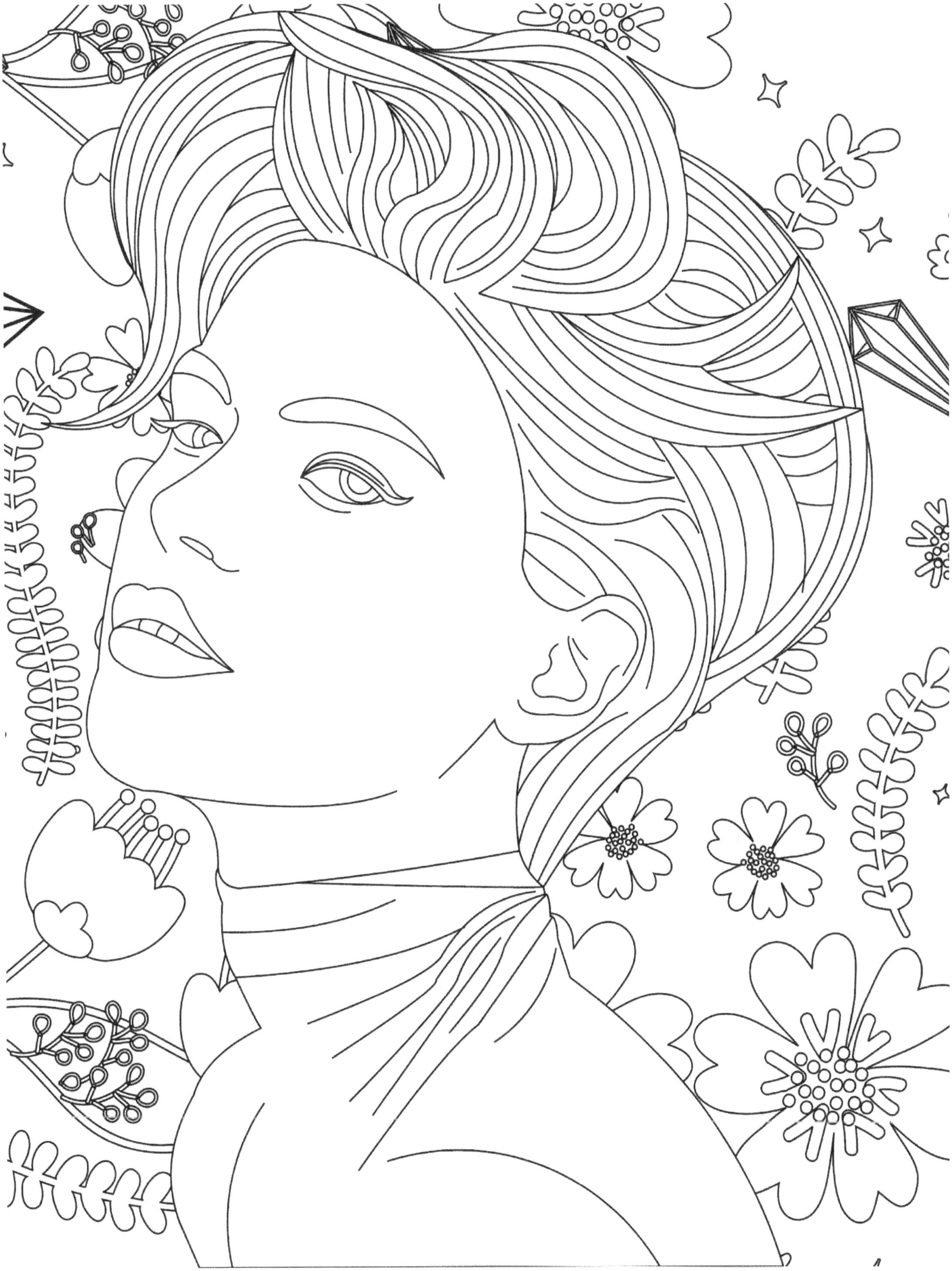

# Bonus

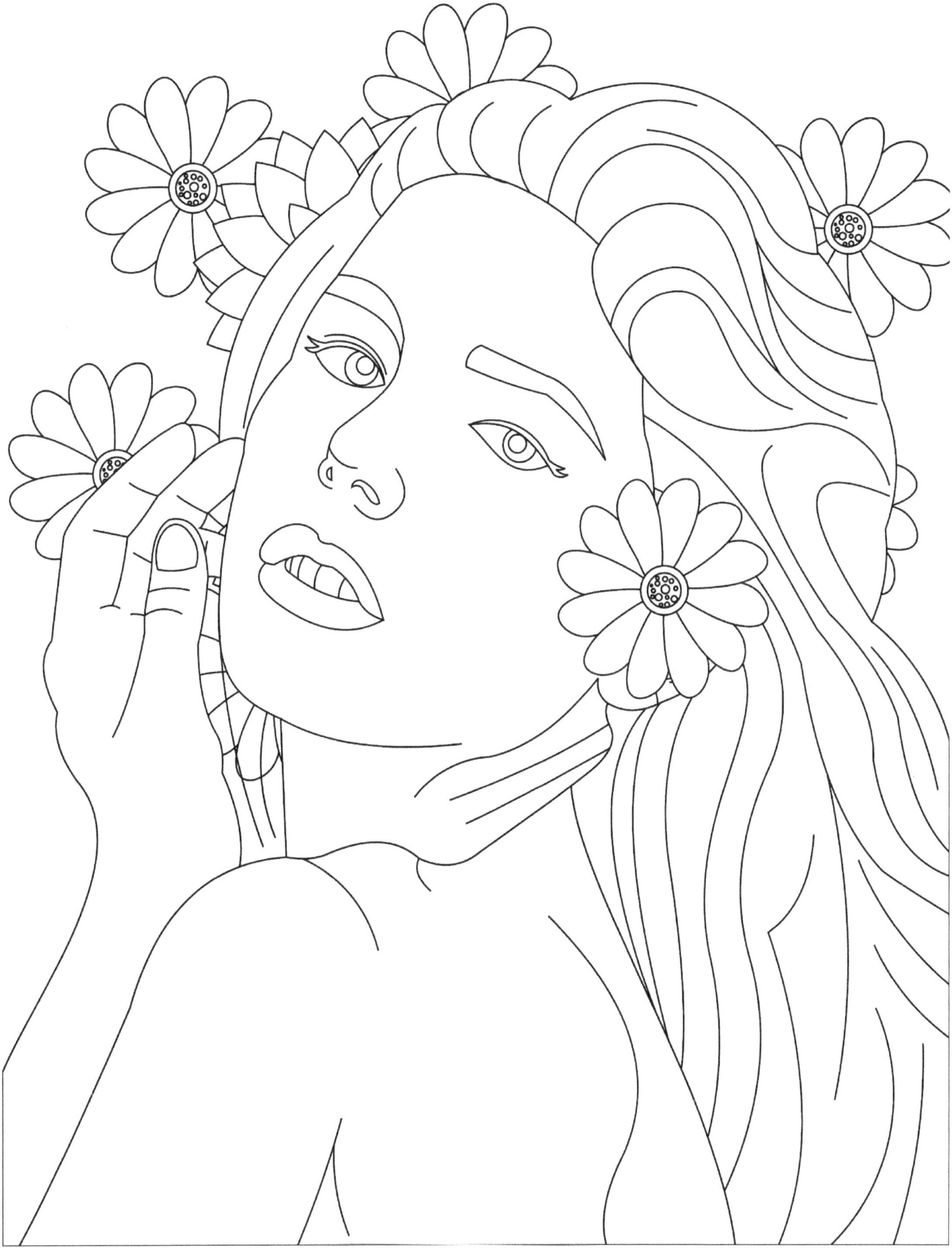

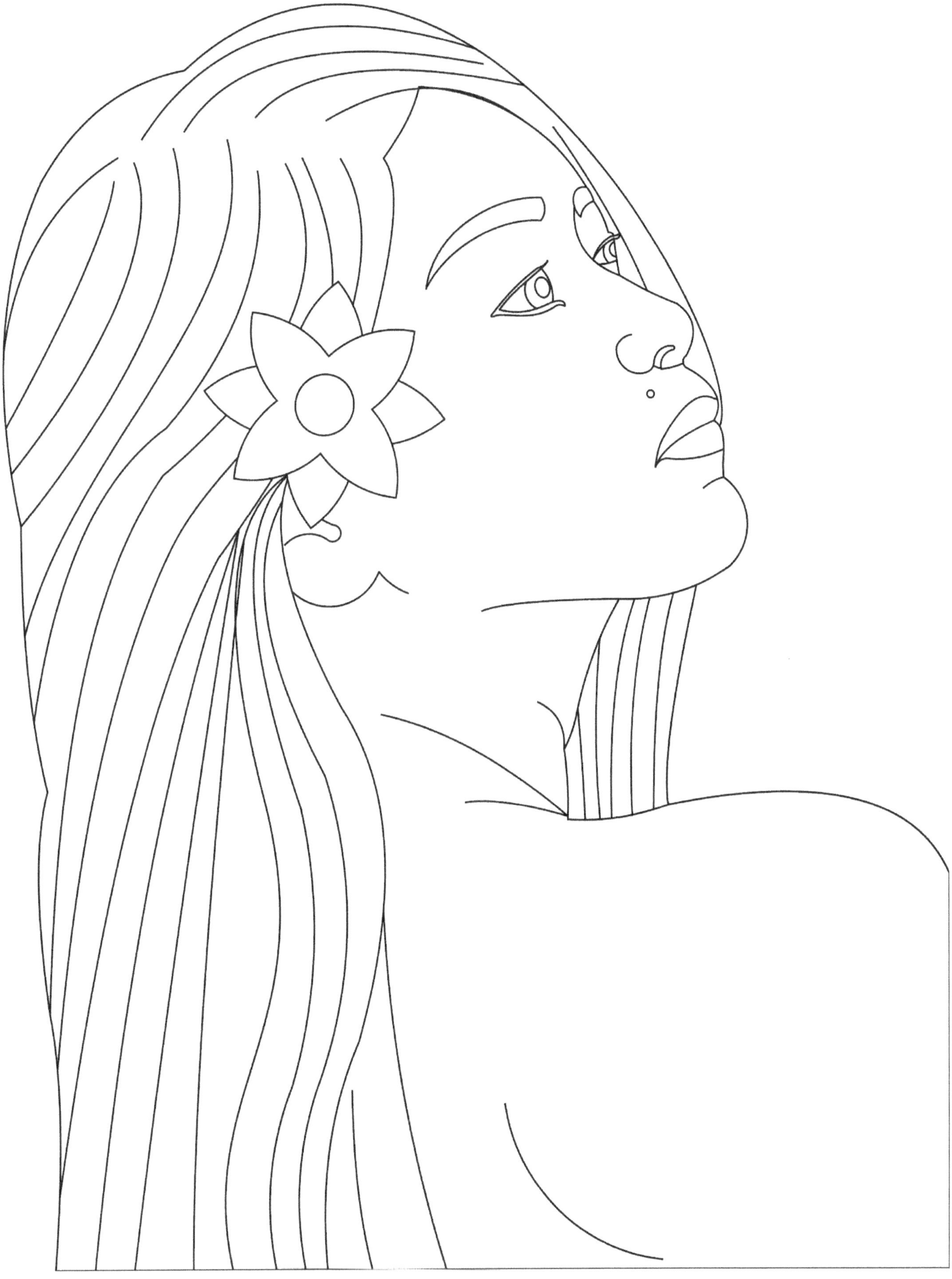

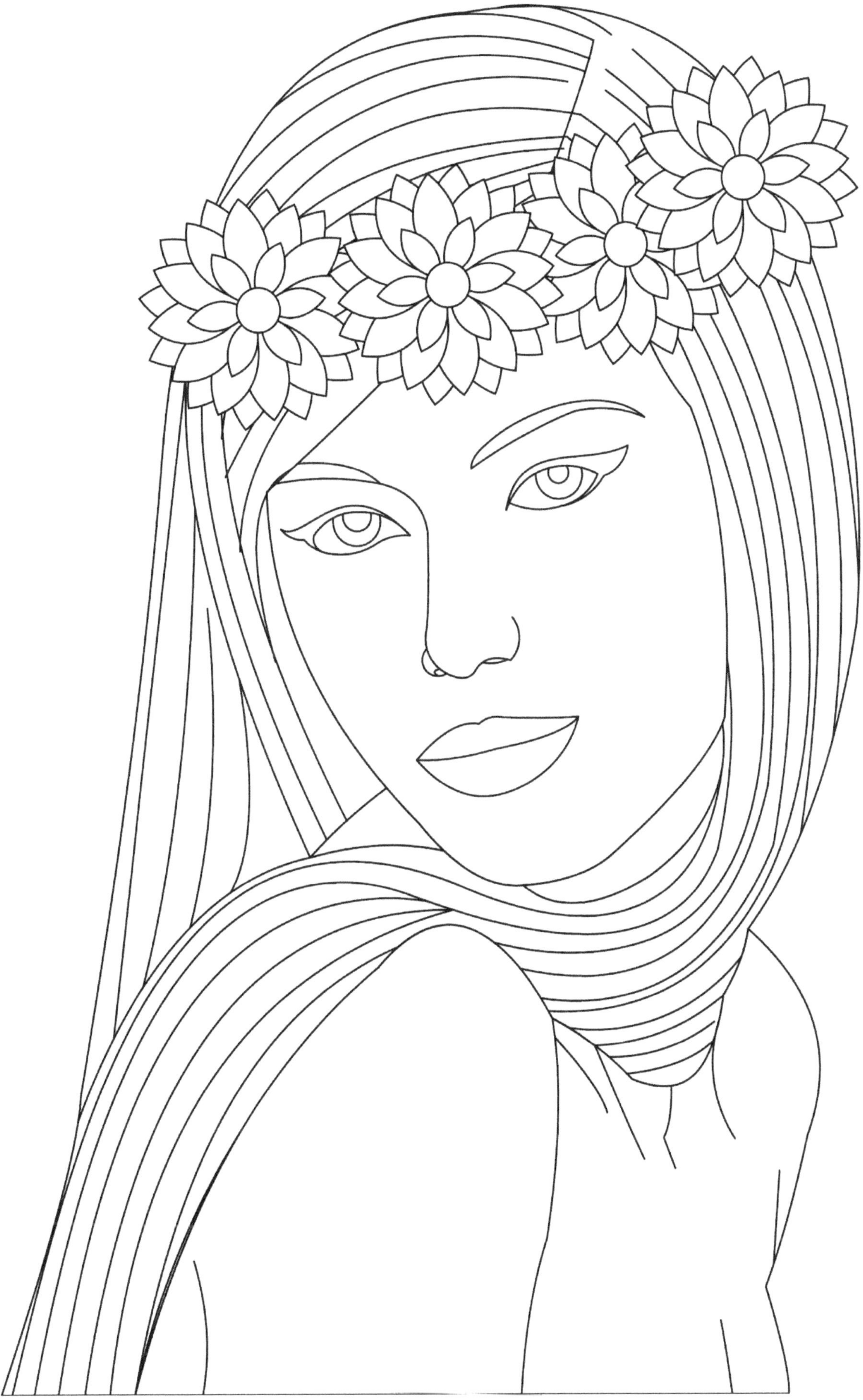

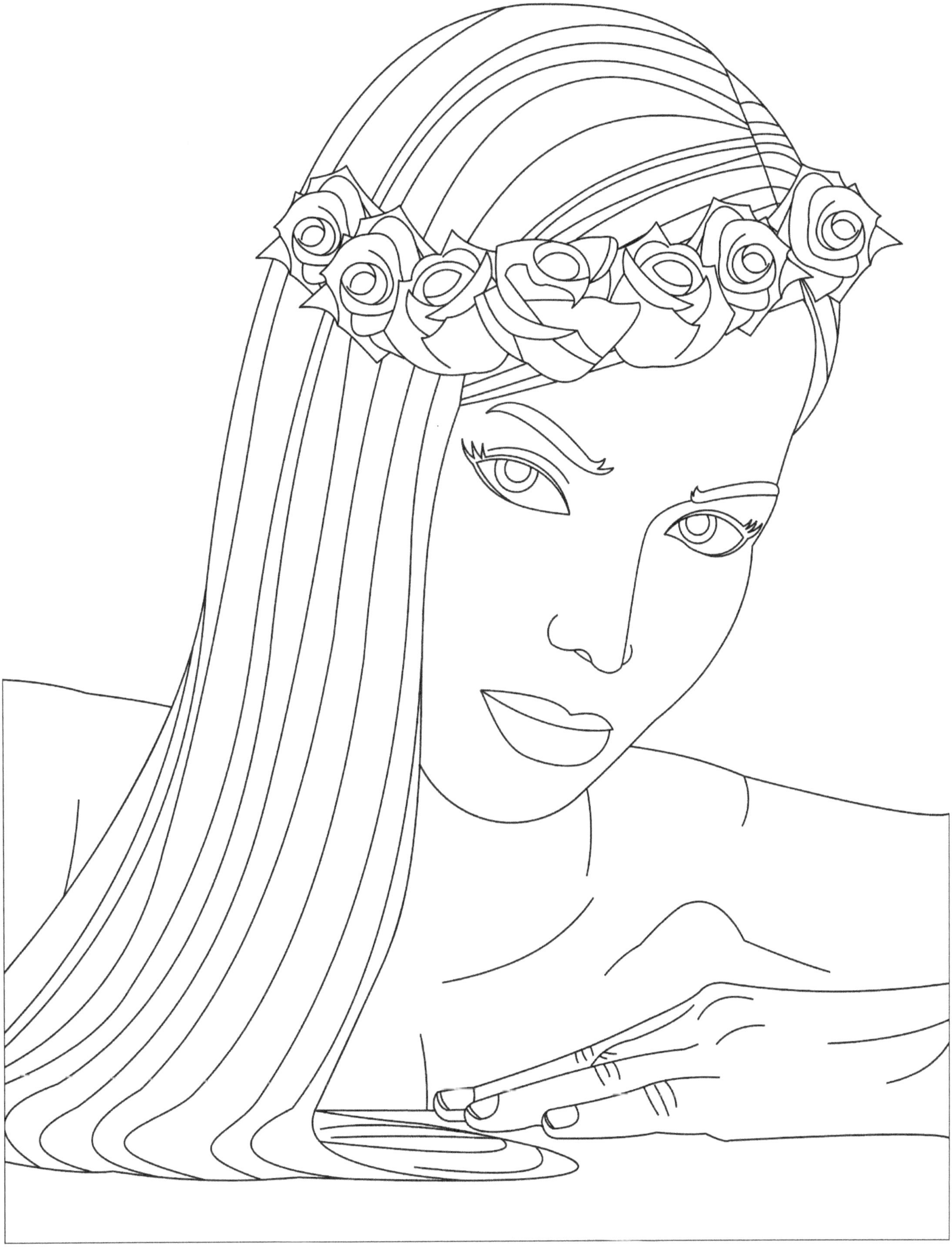

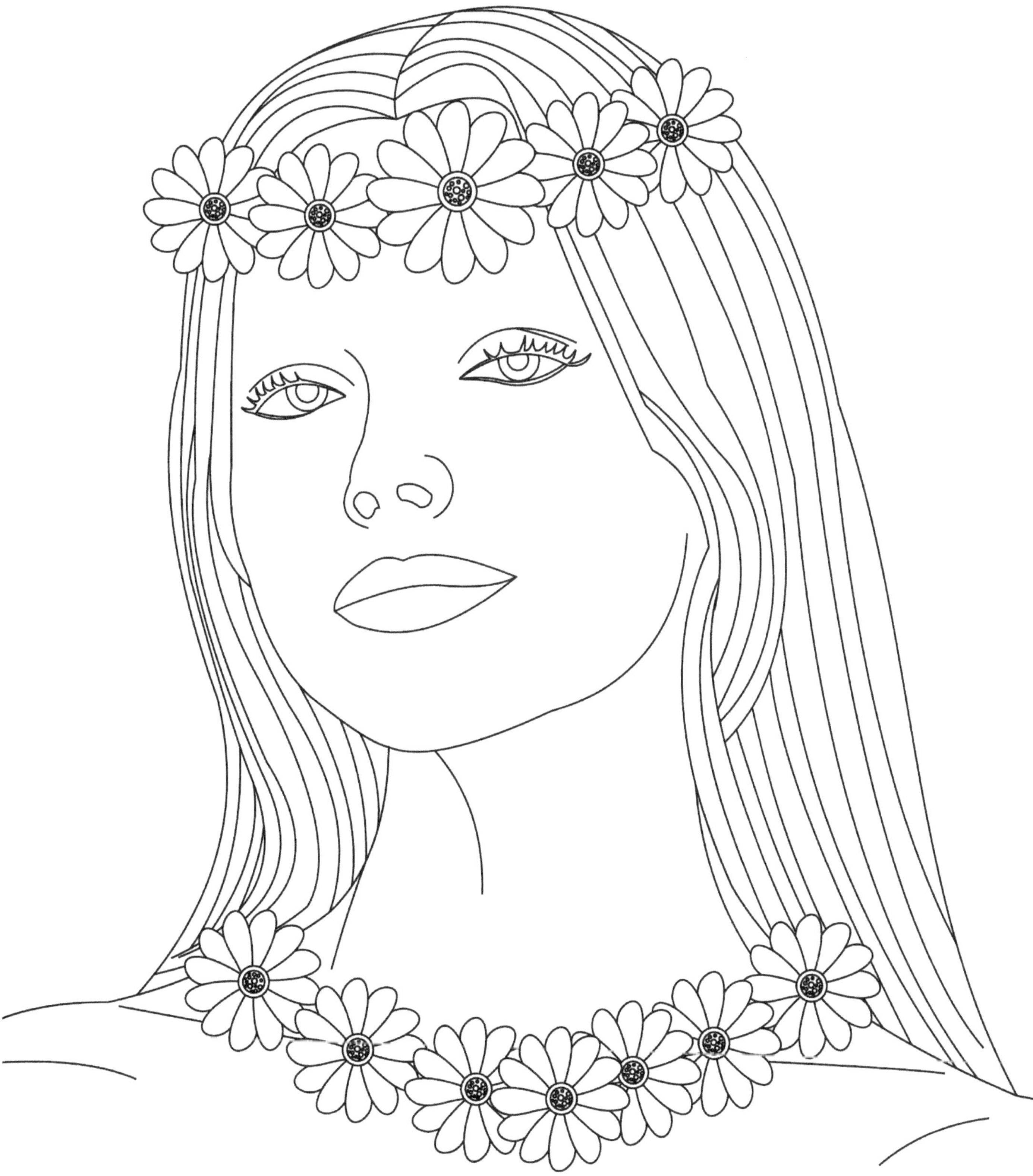

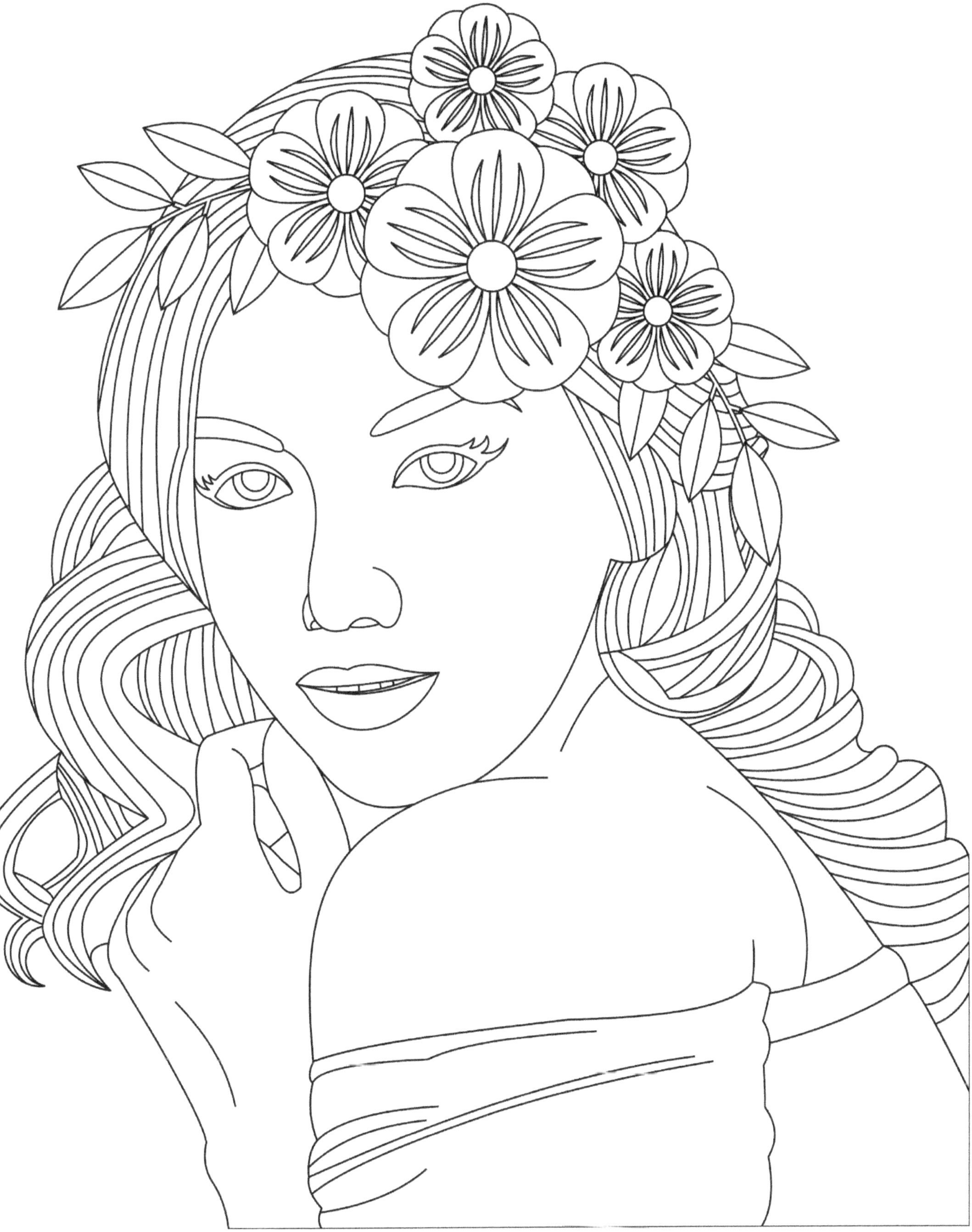

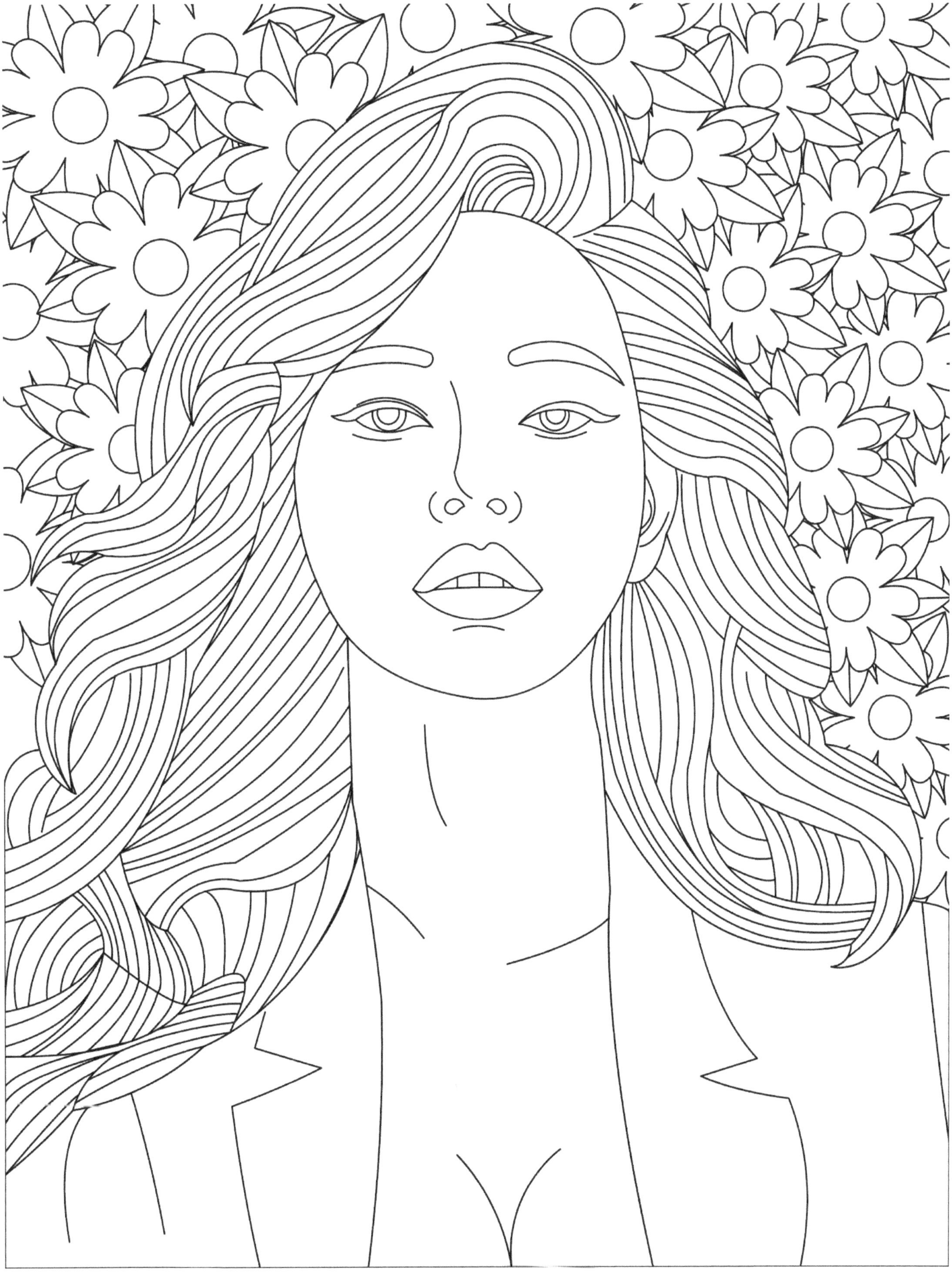

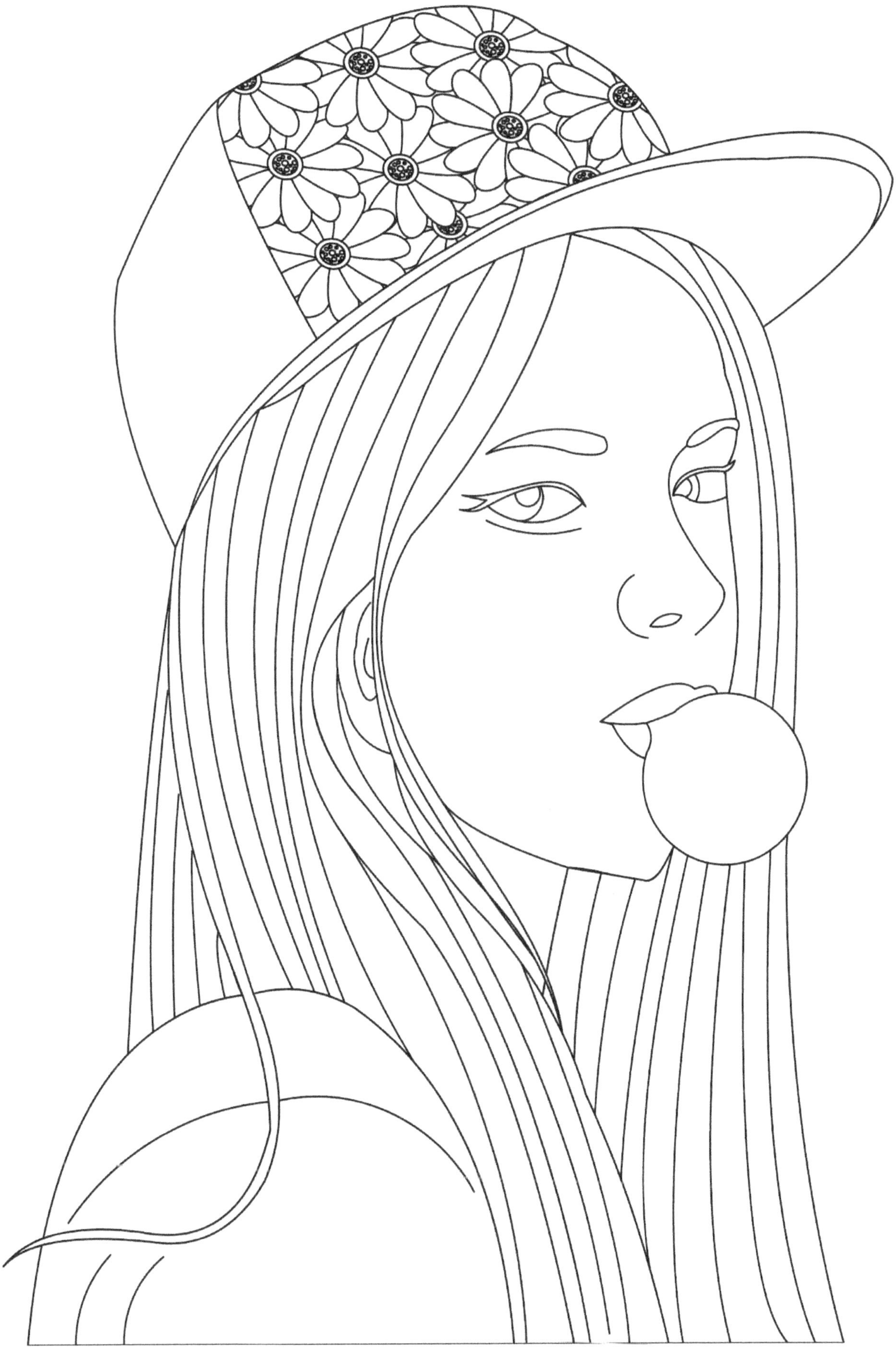

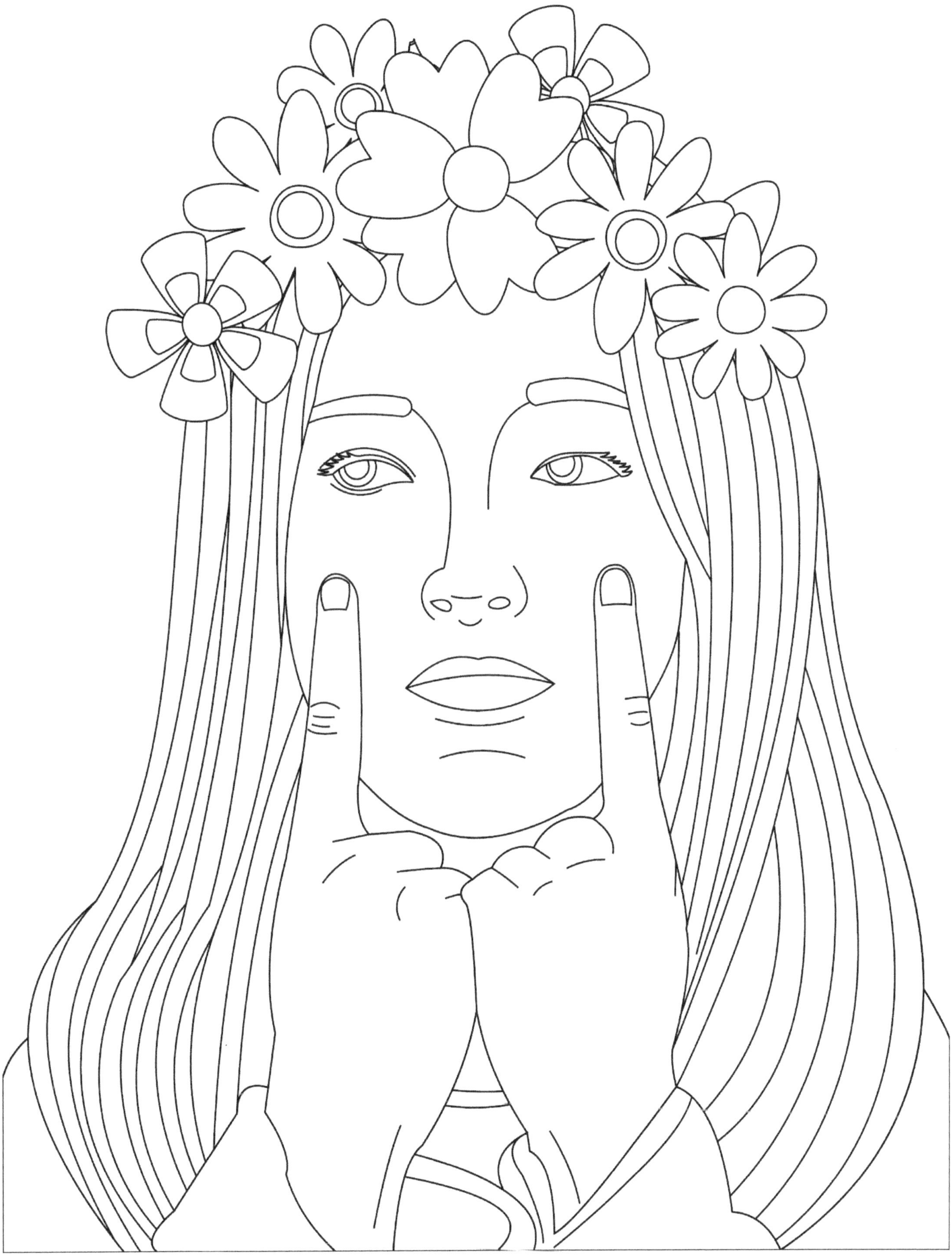

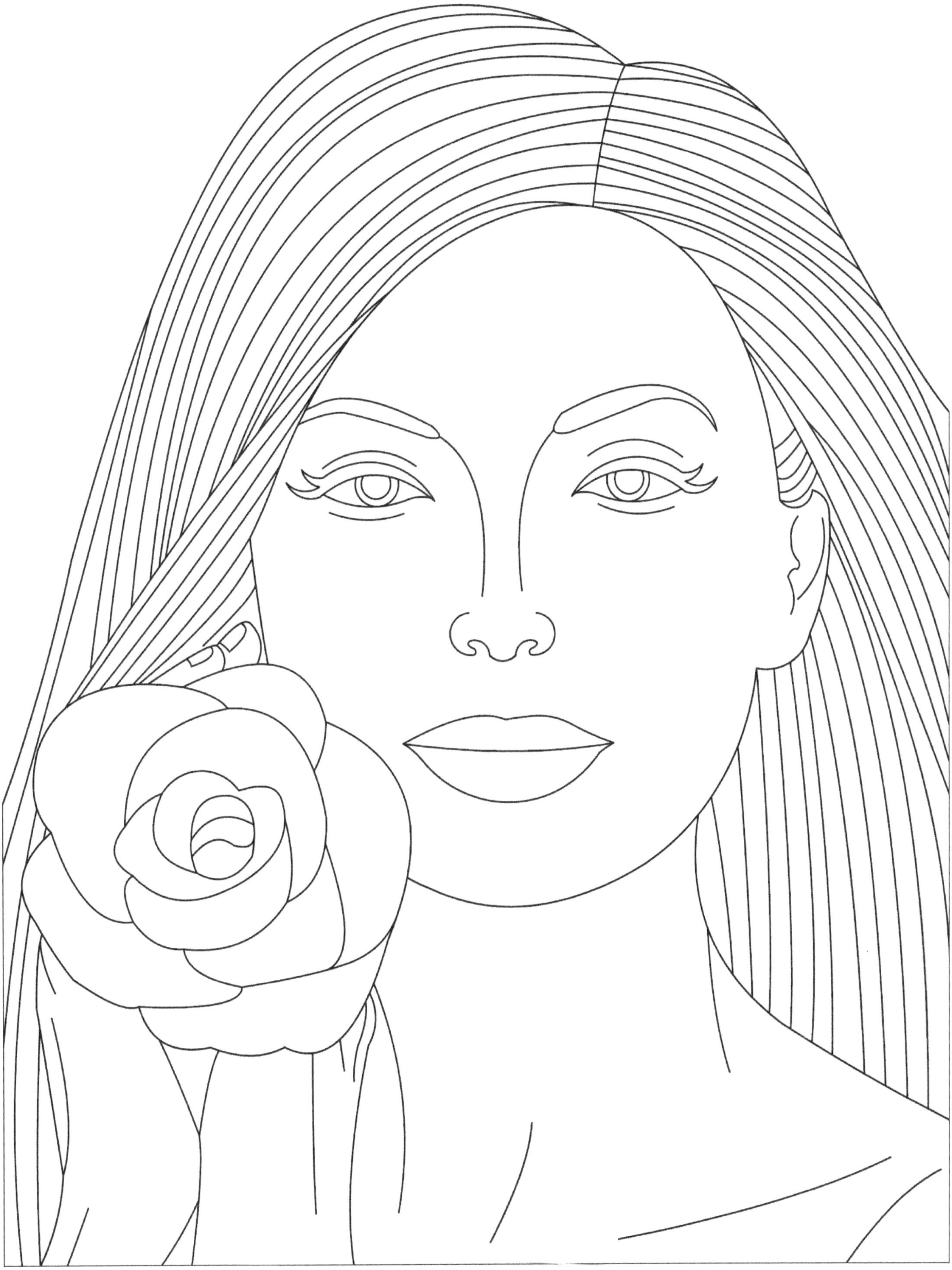

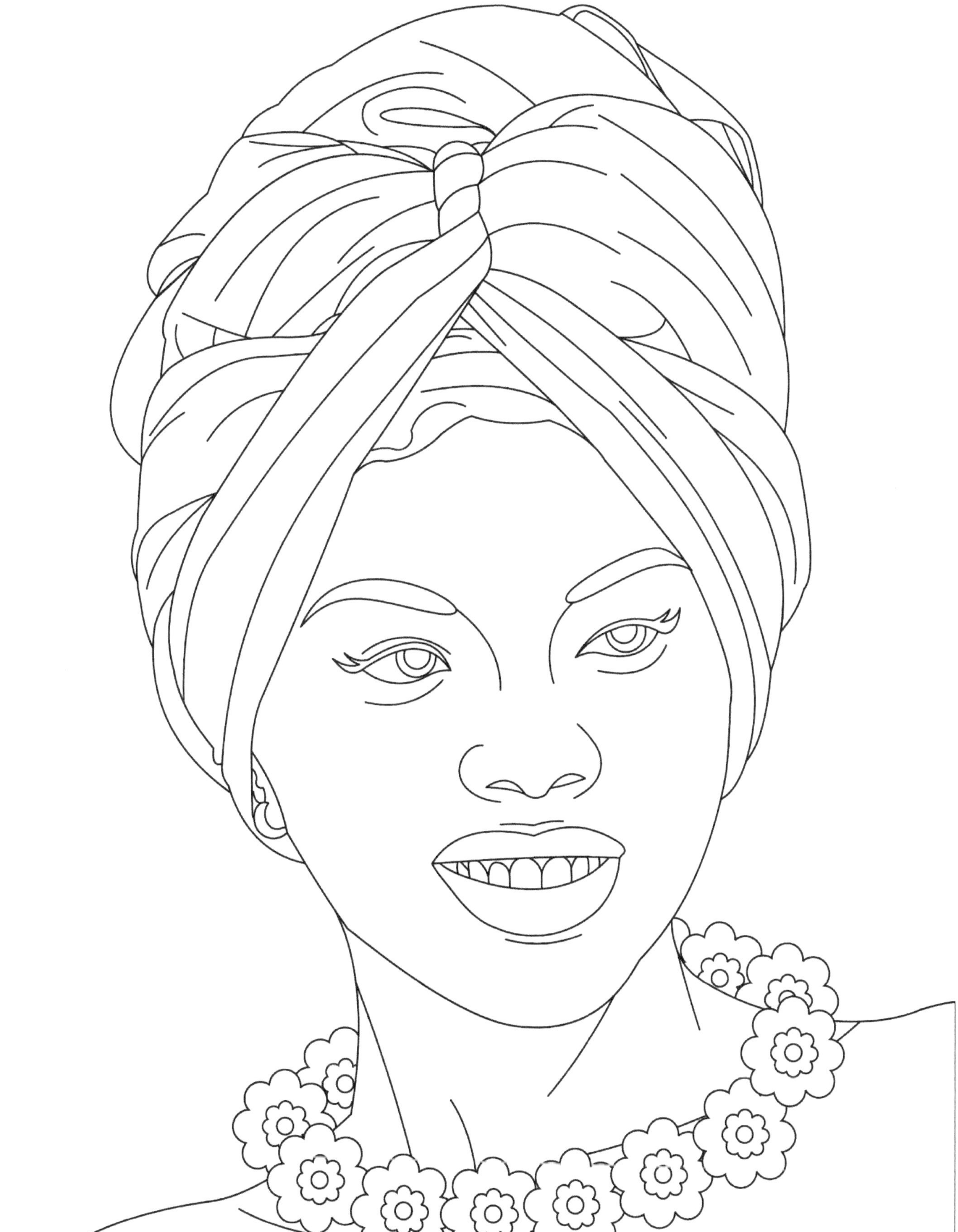

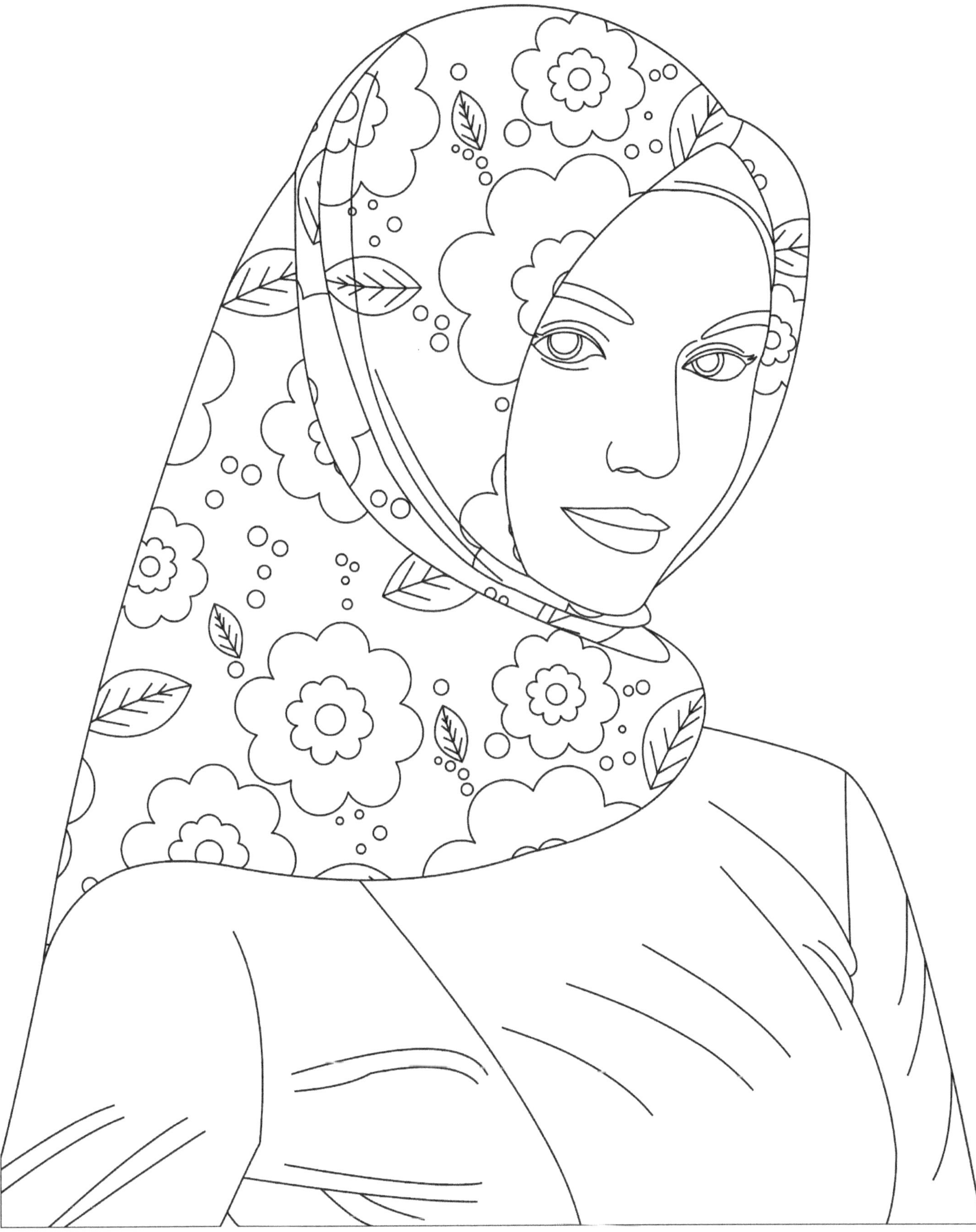

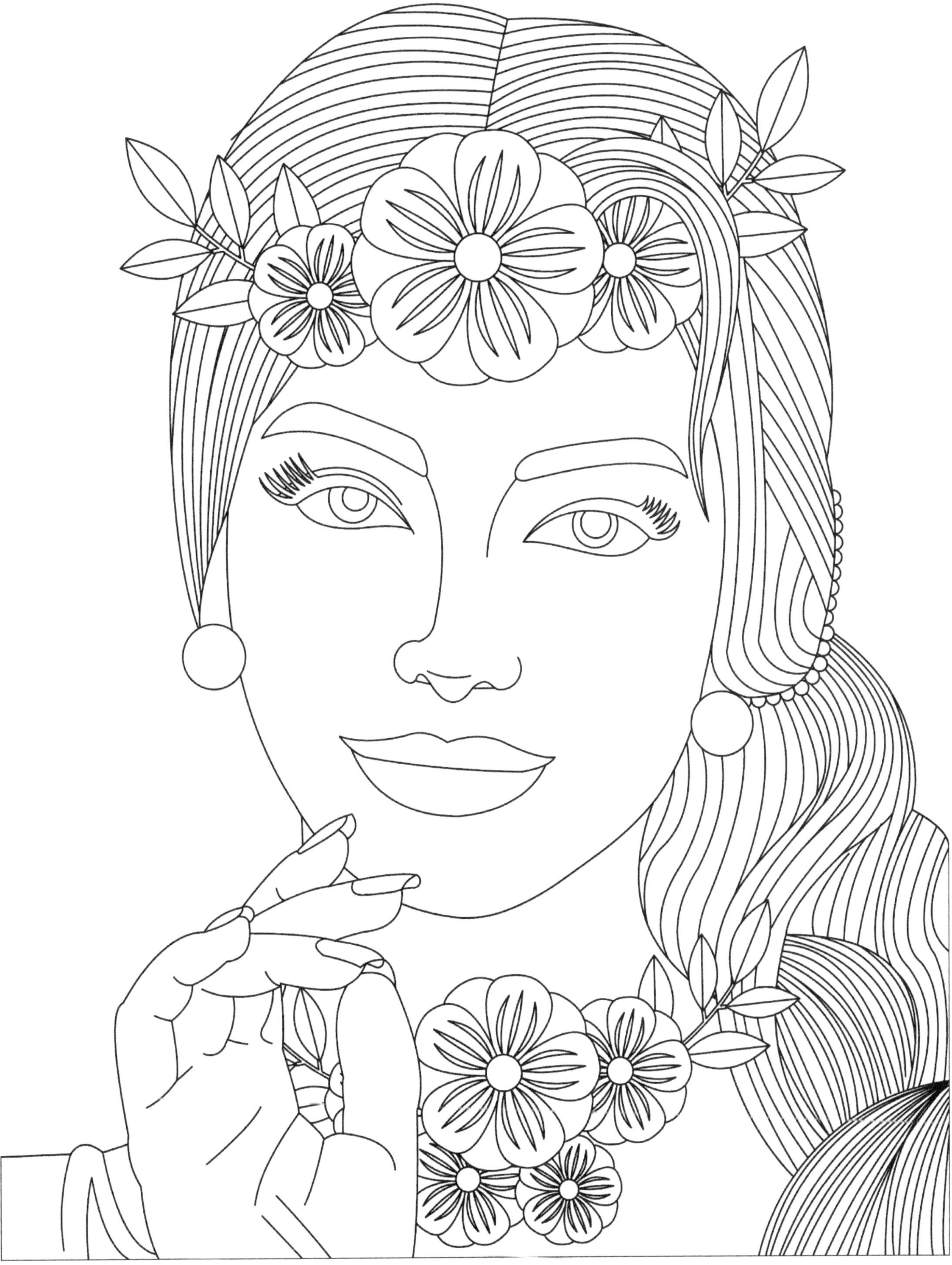

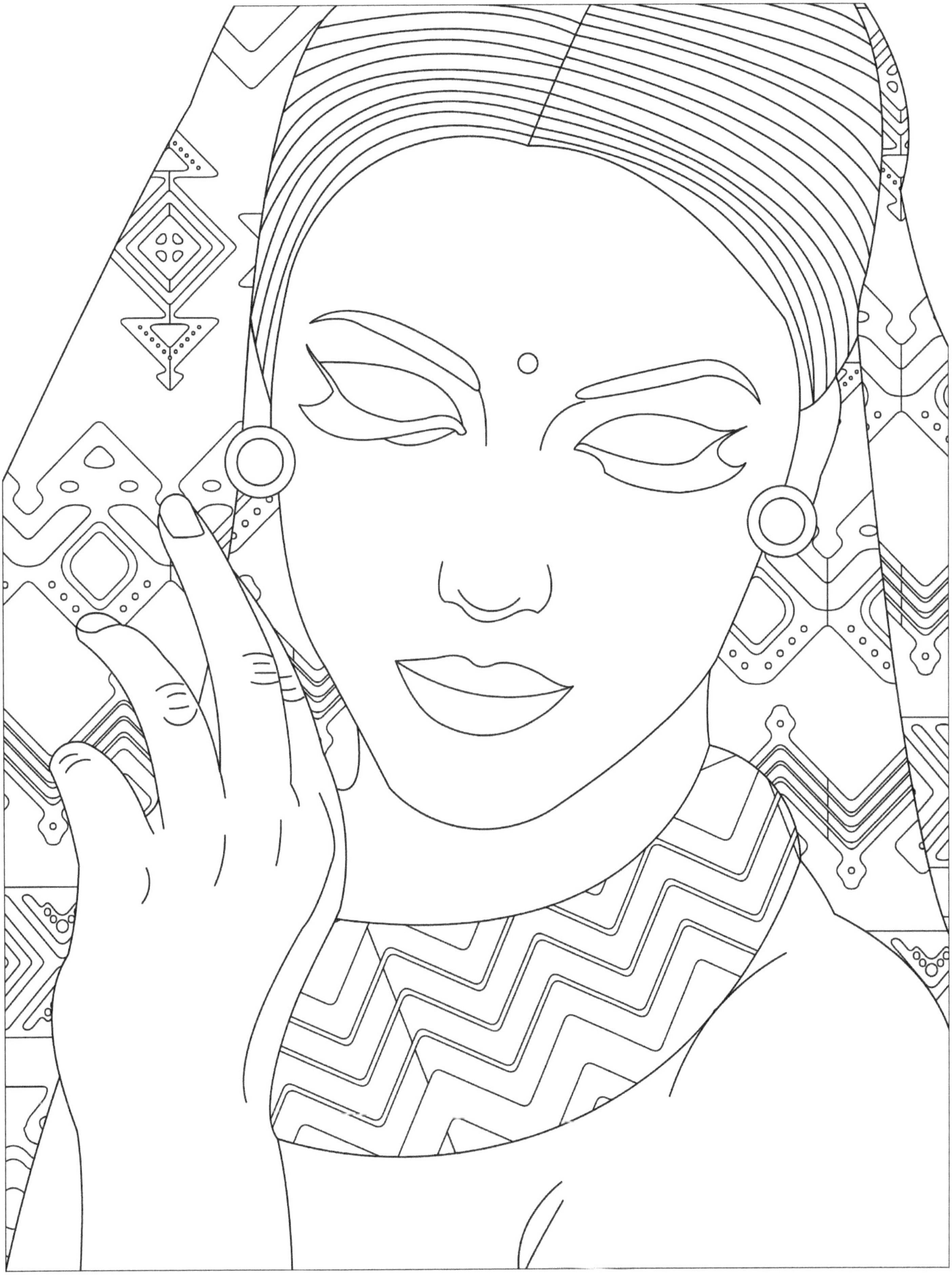

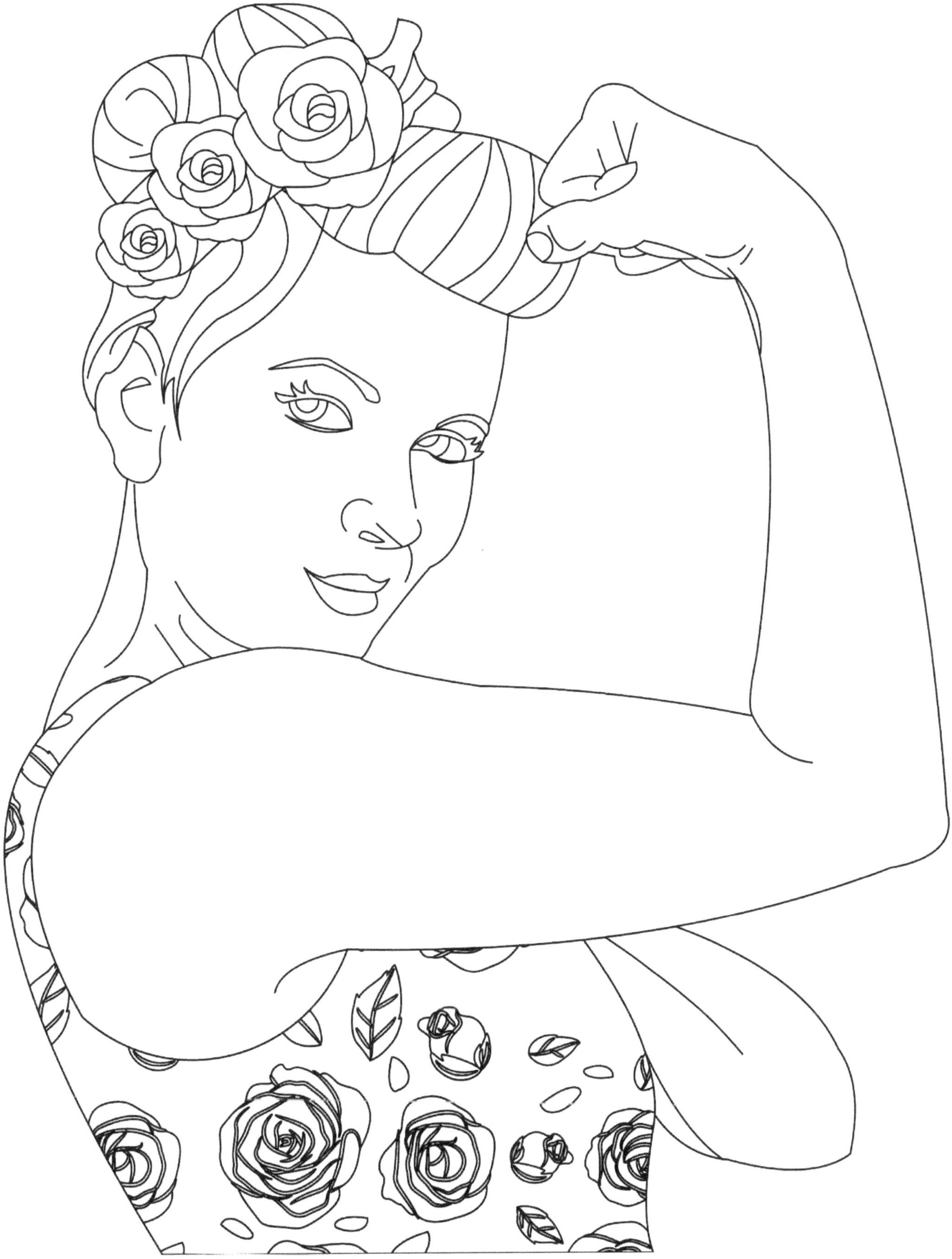

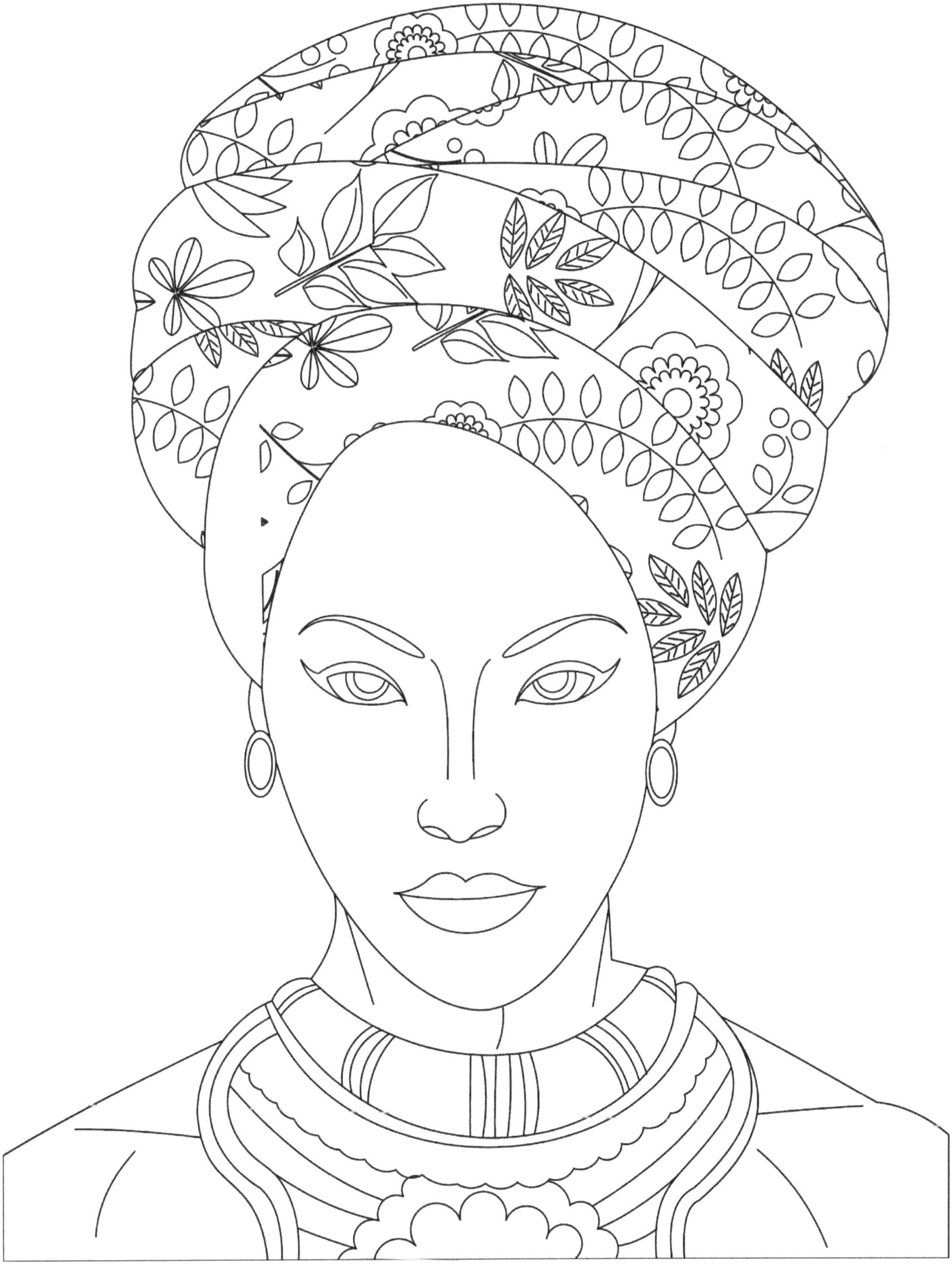

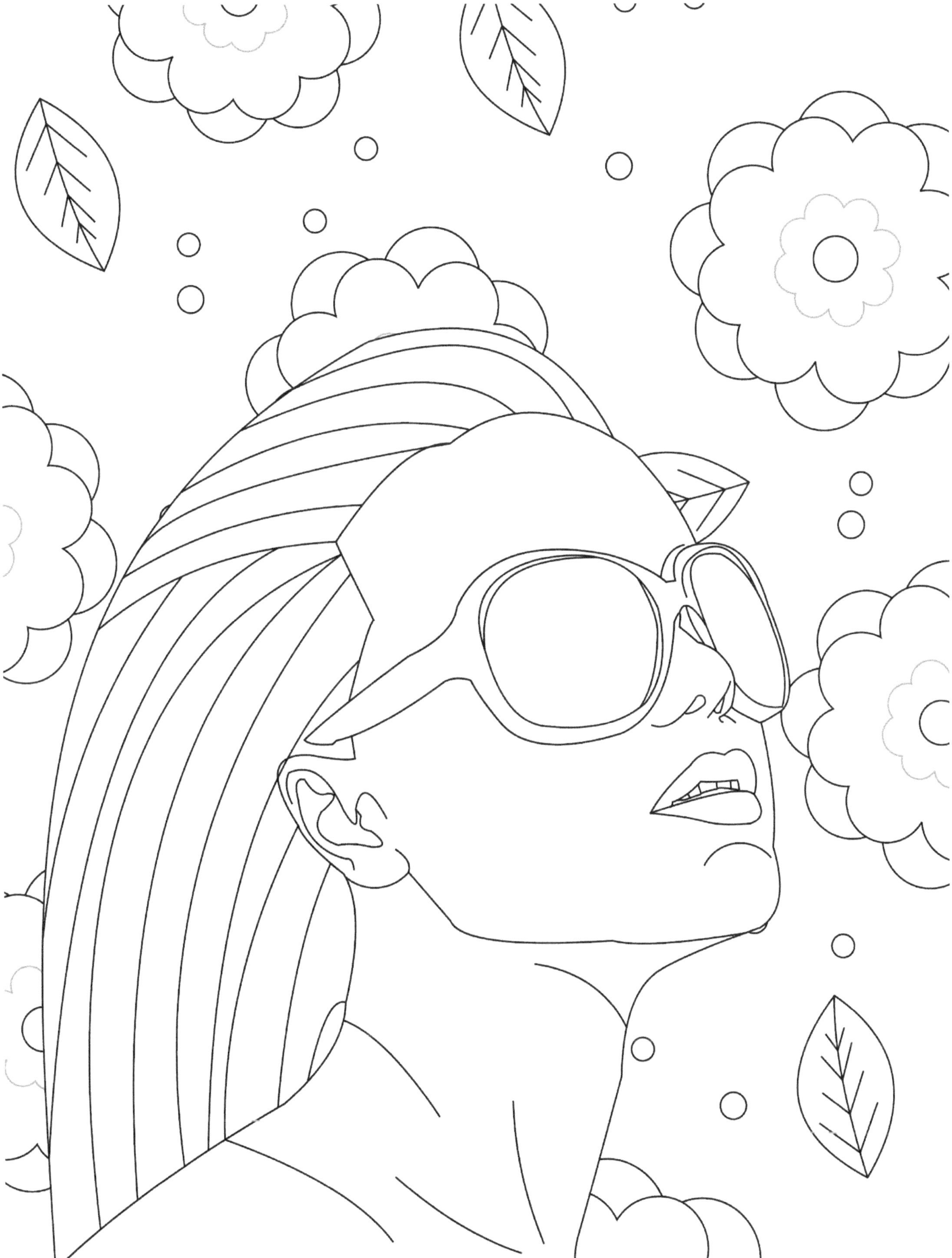

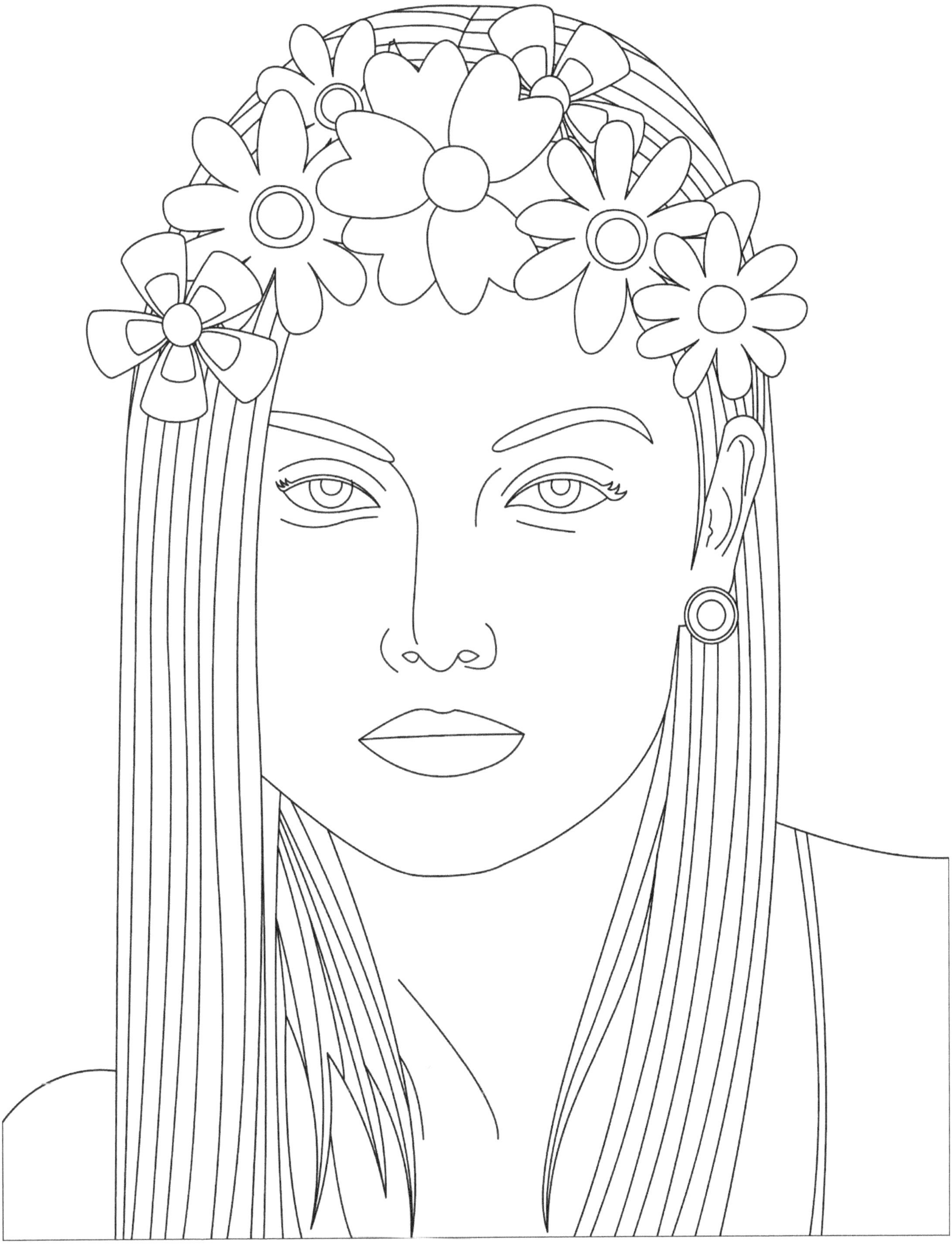

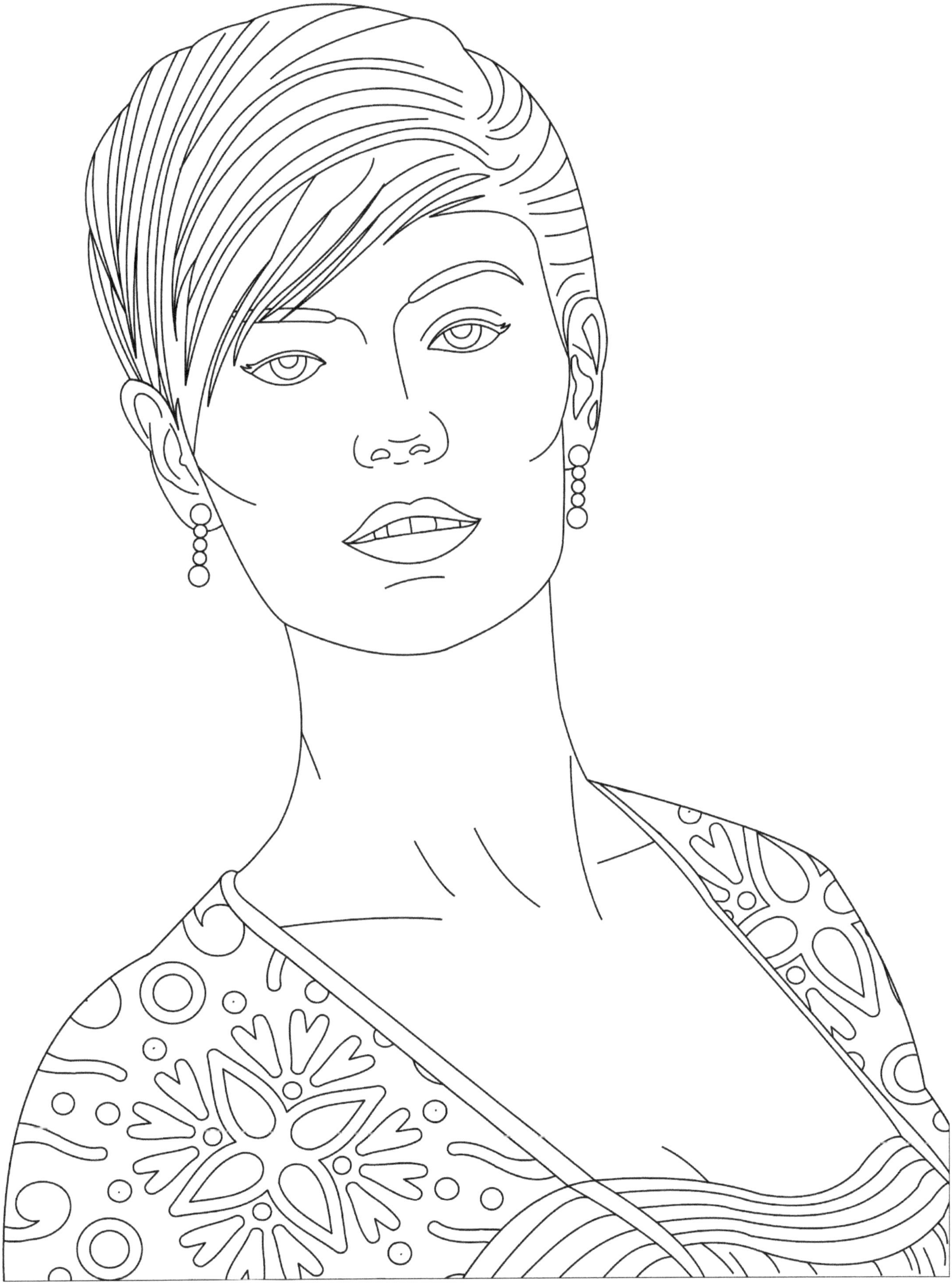

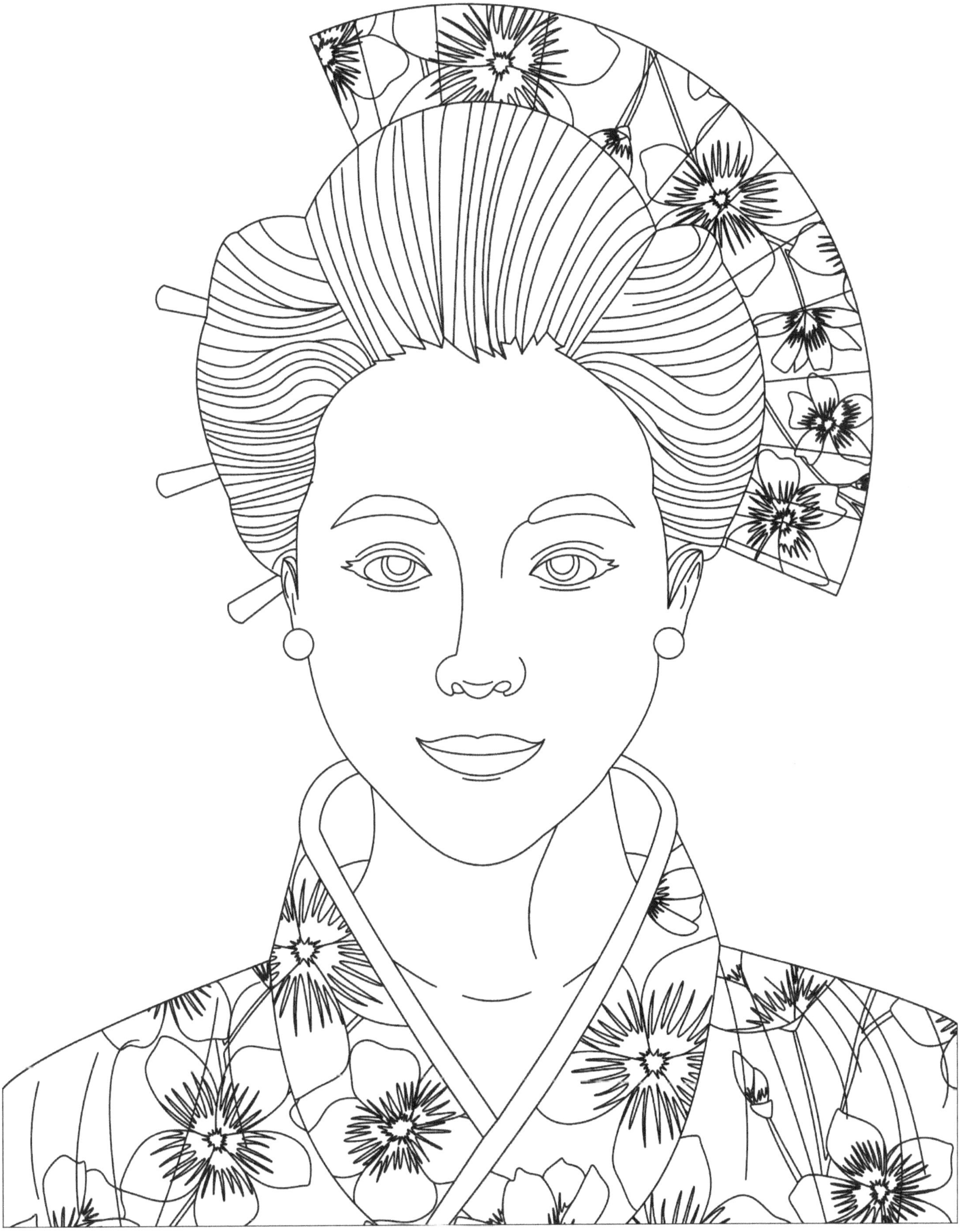

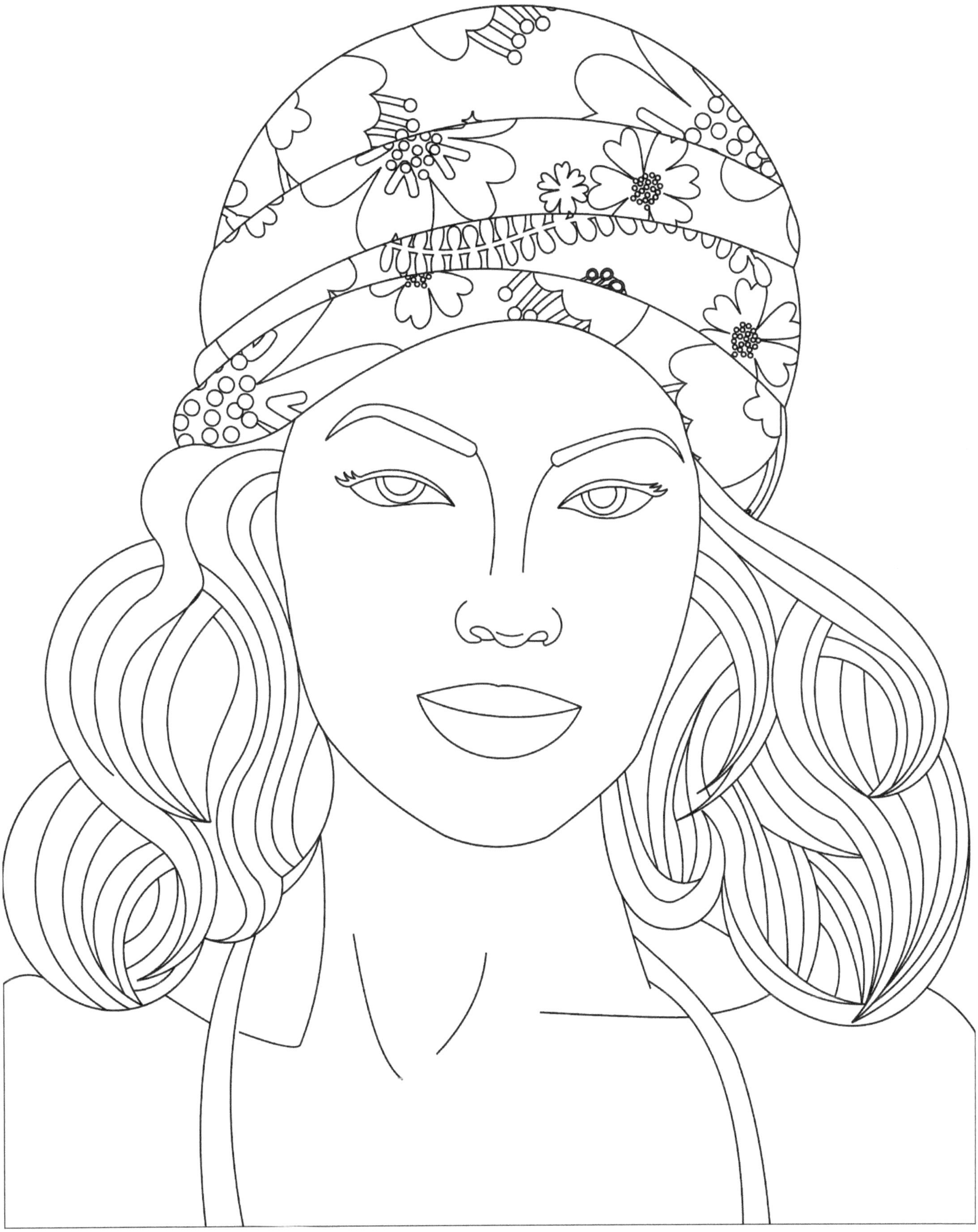

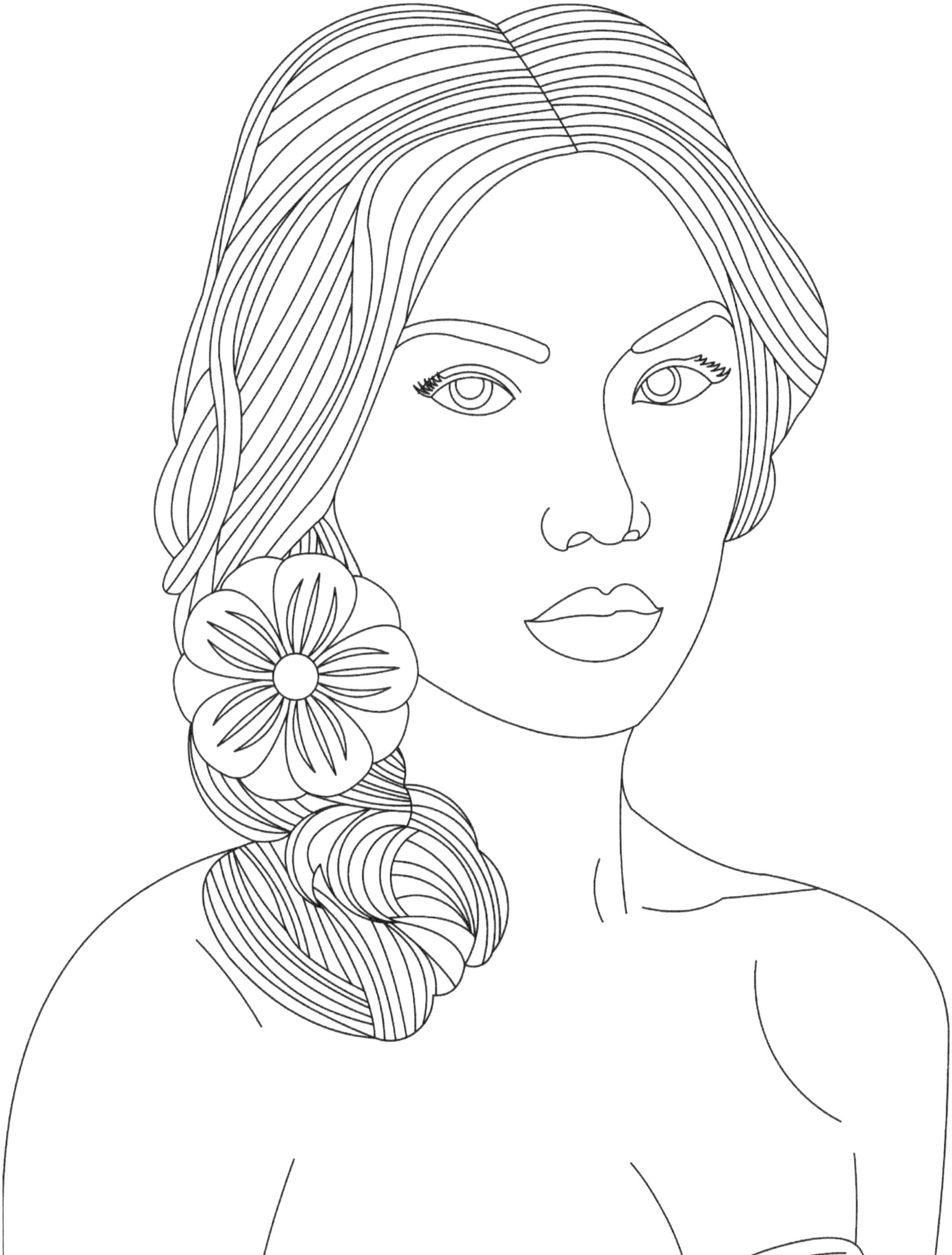

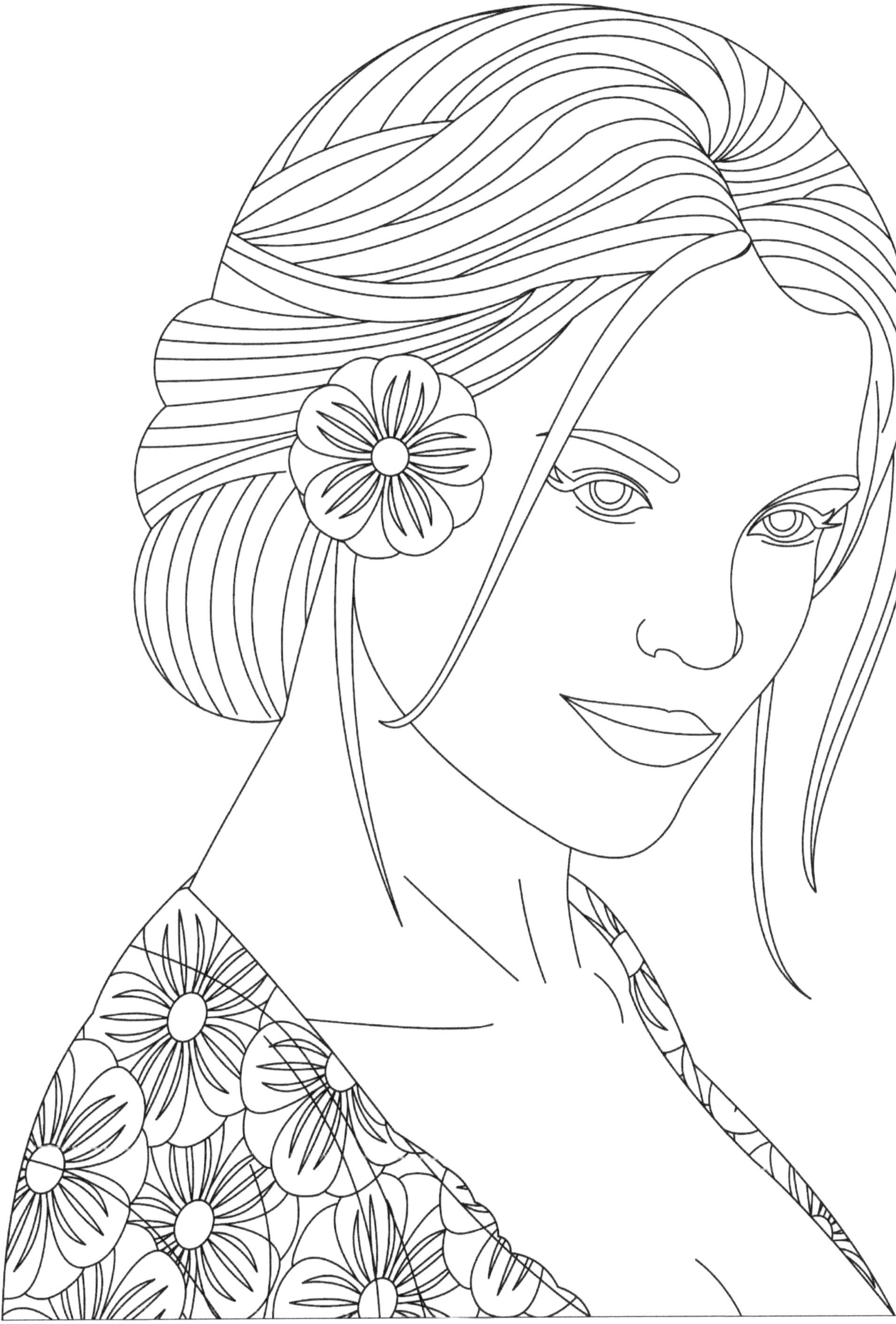

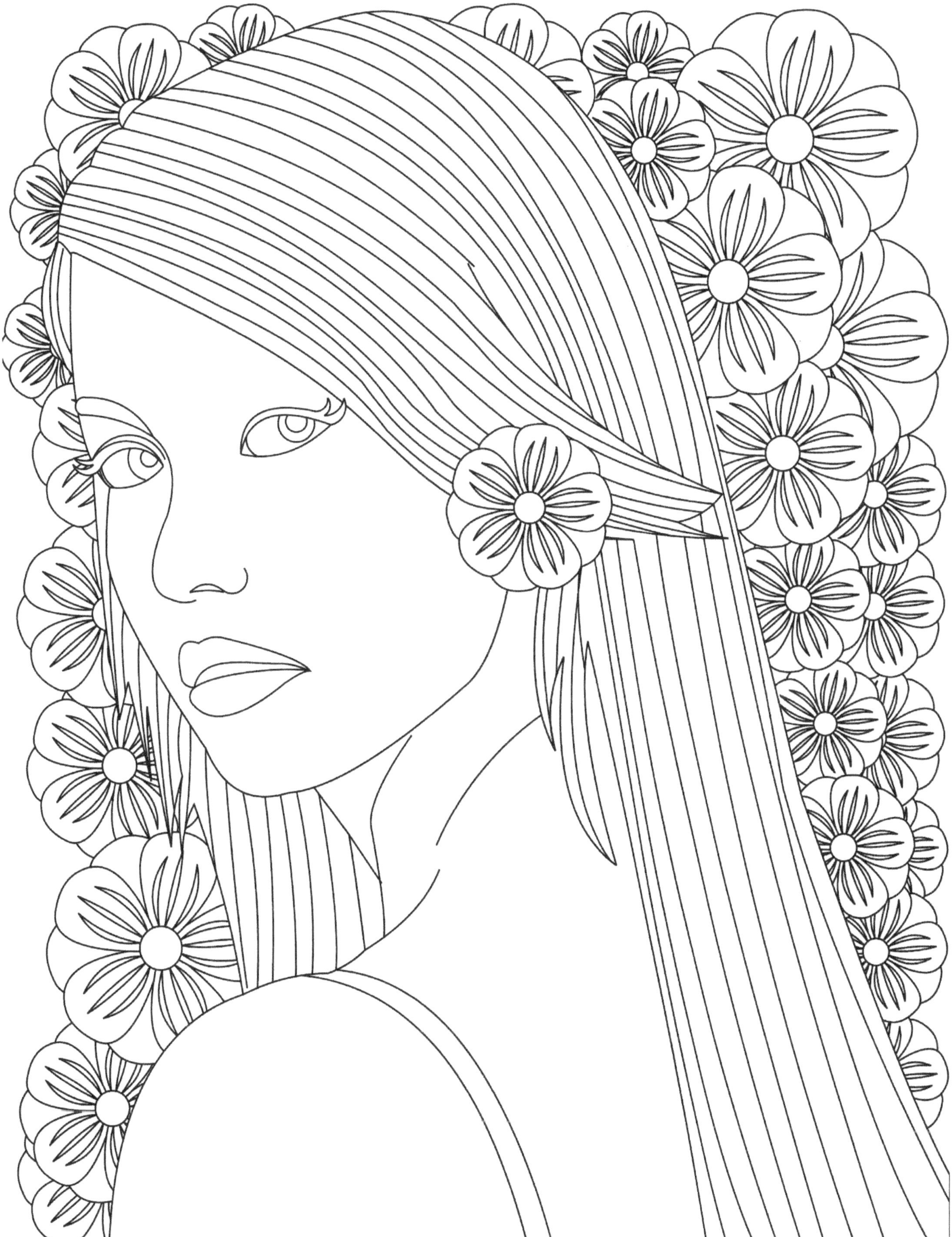

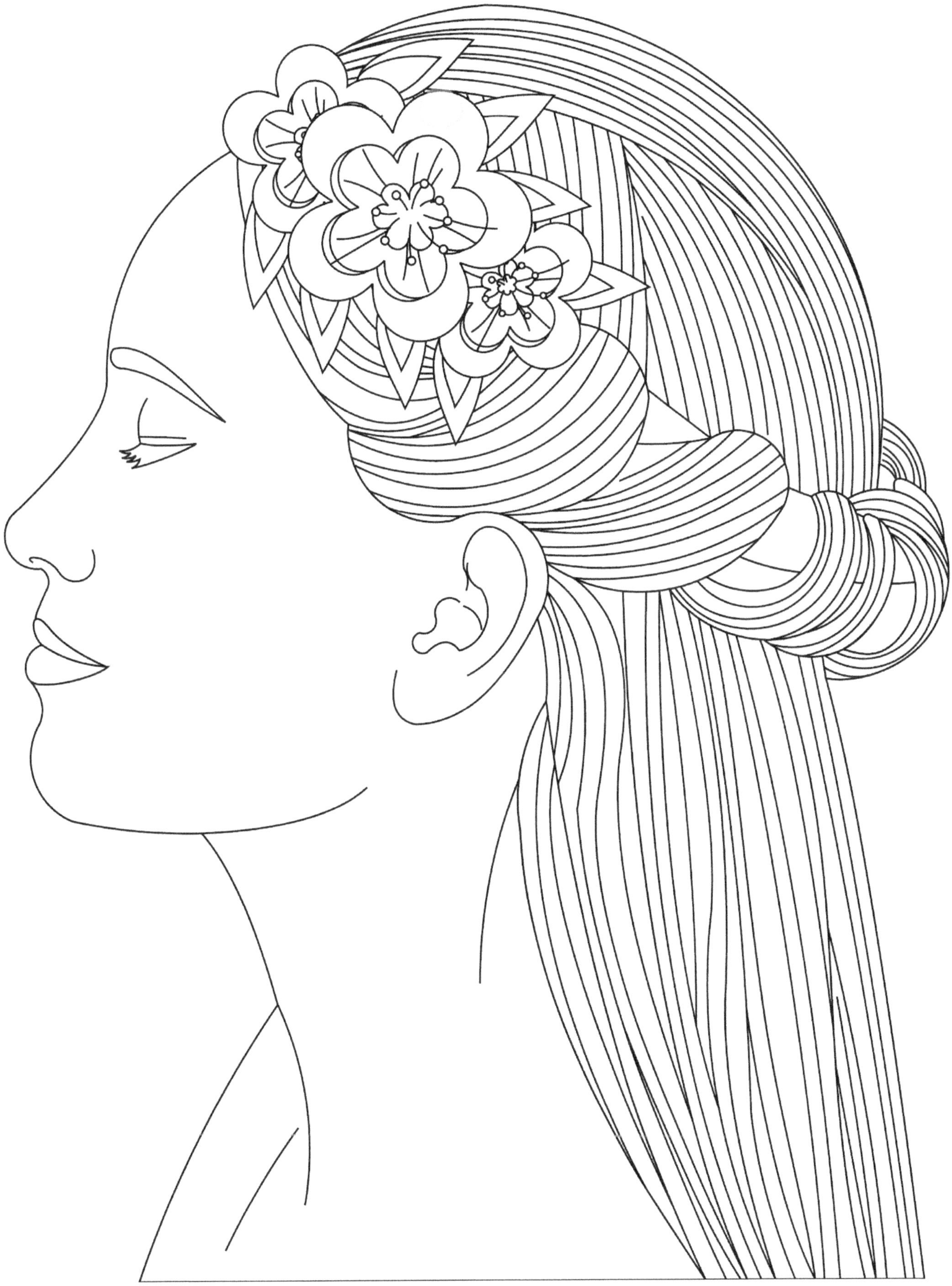

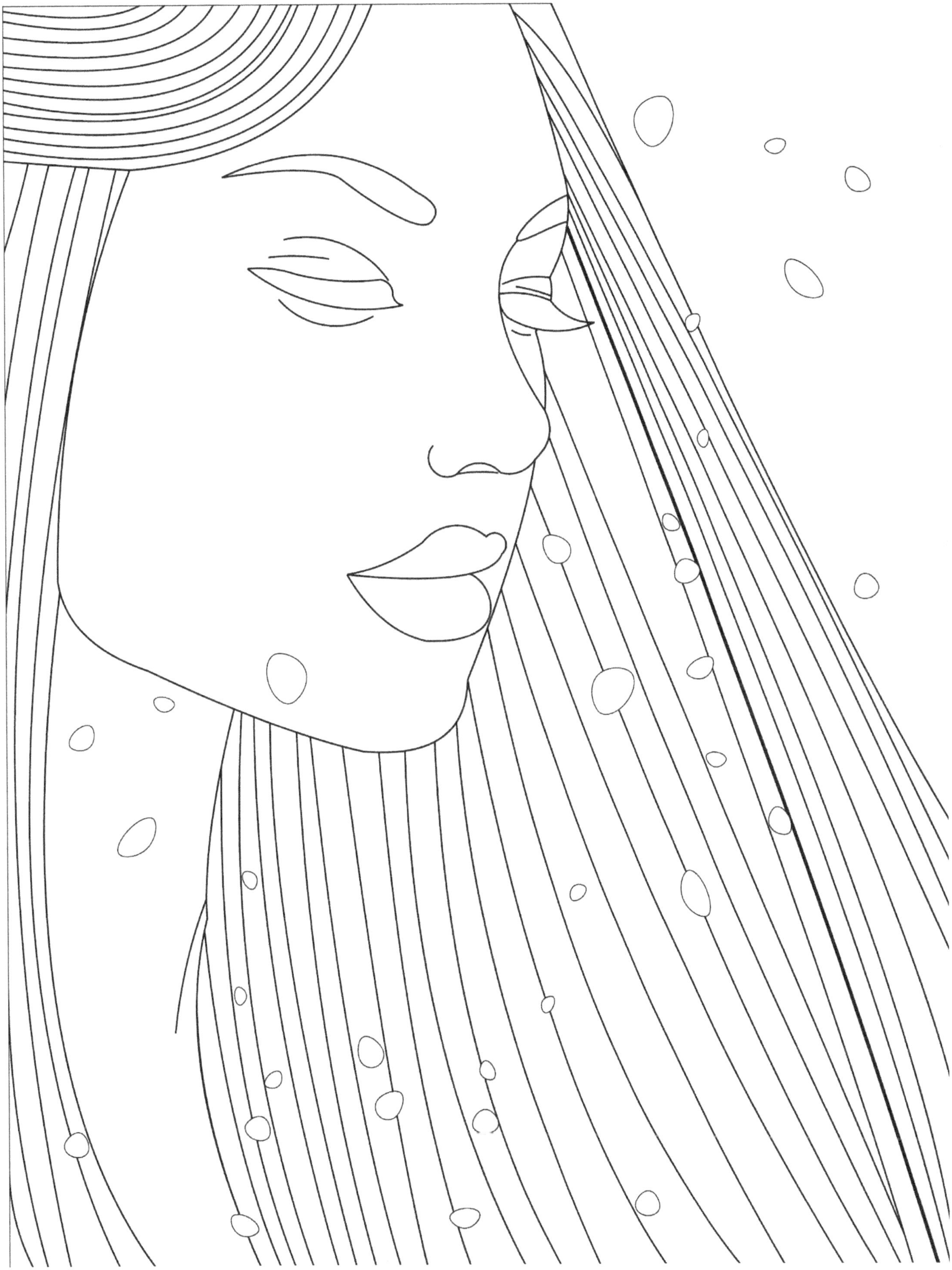

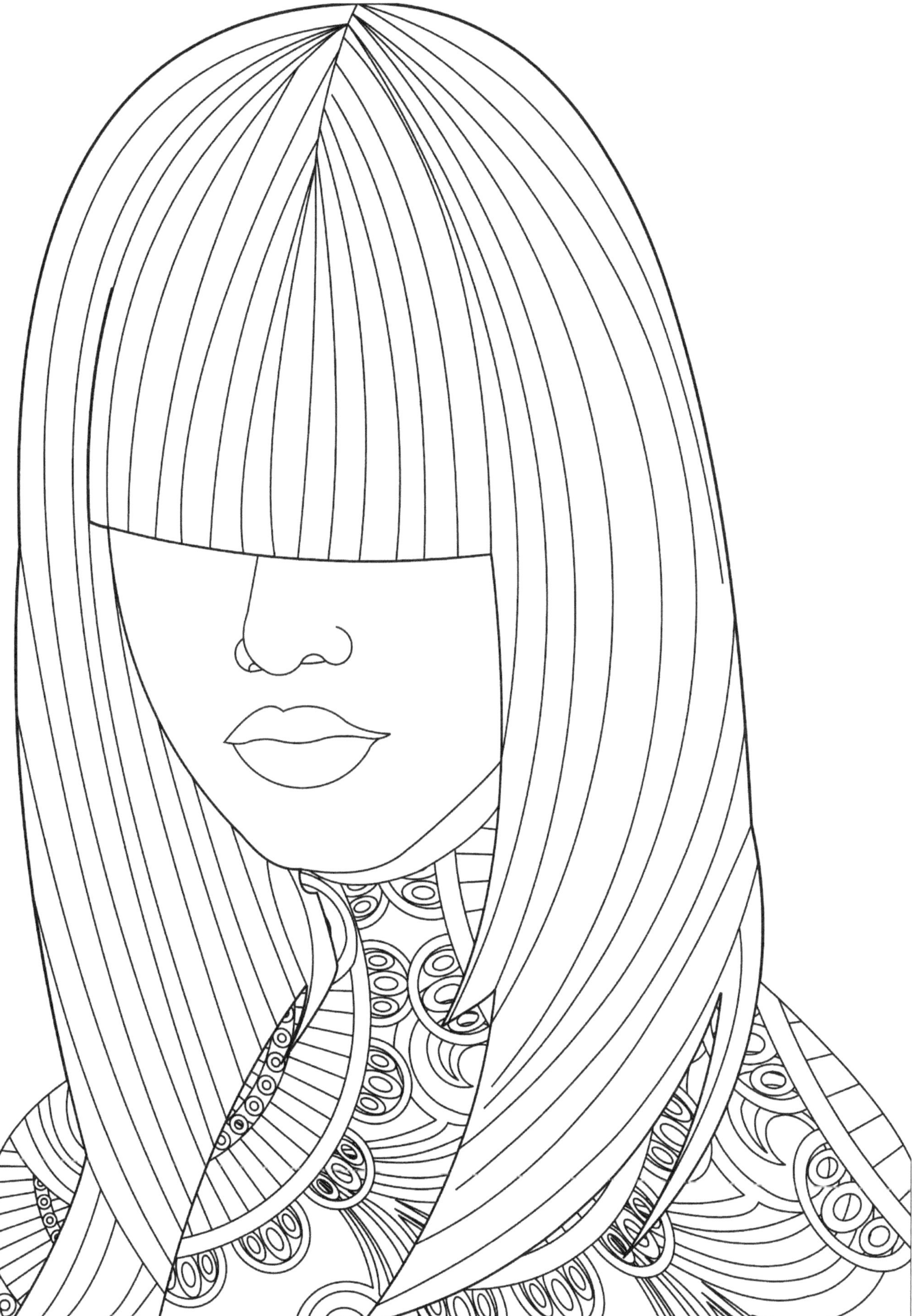

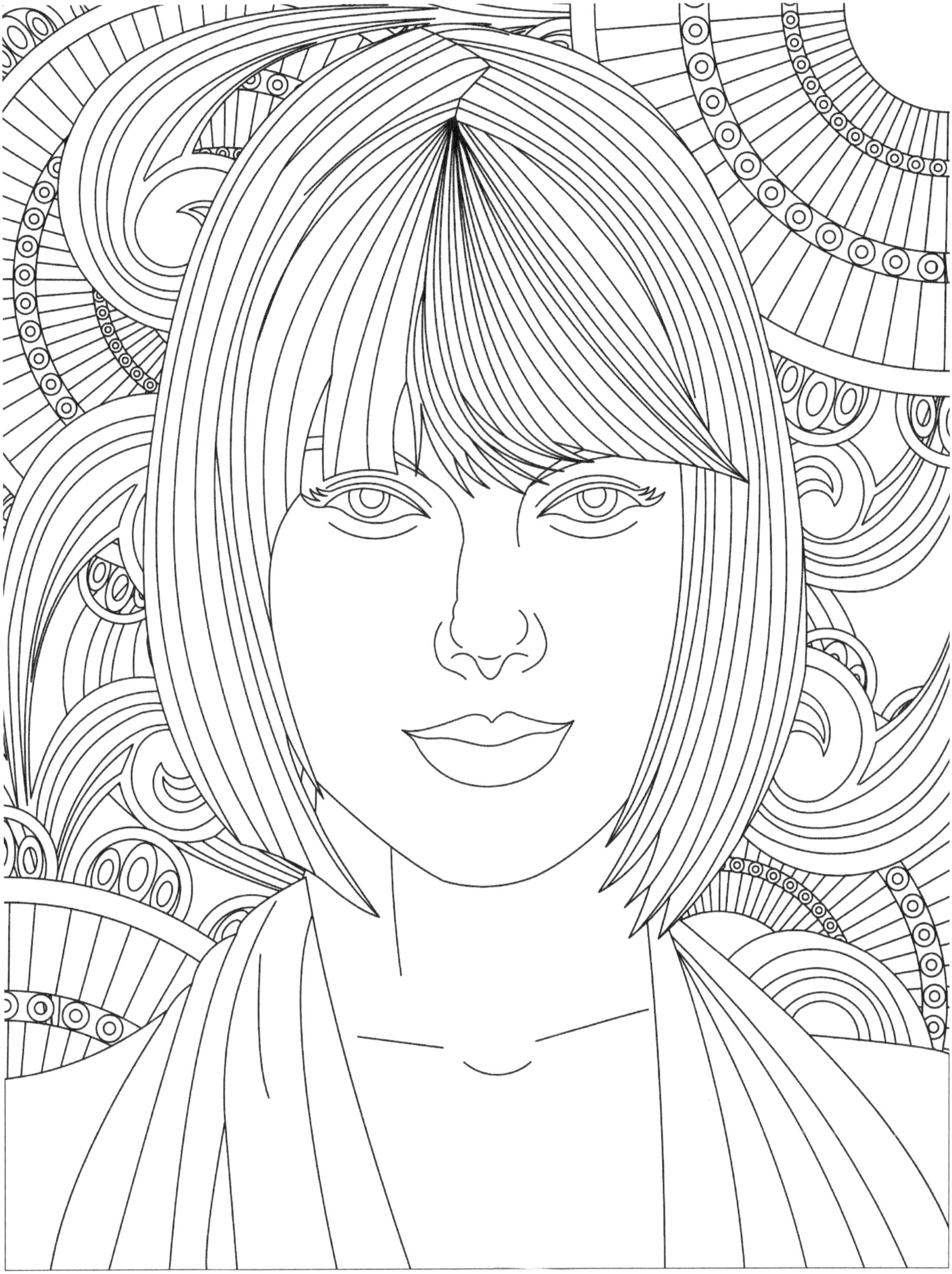

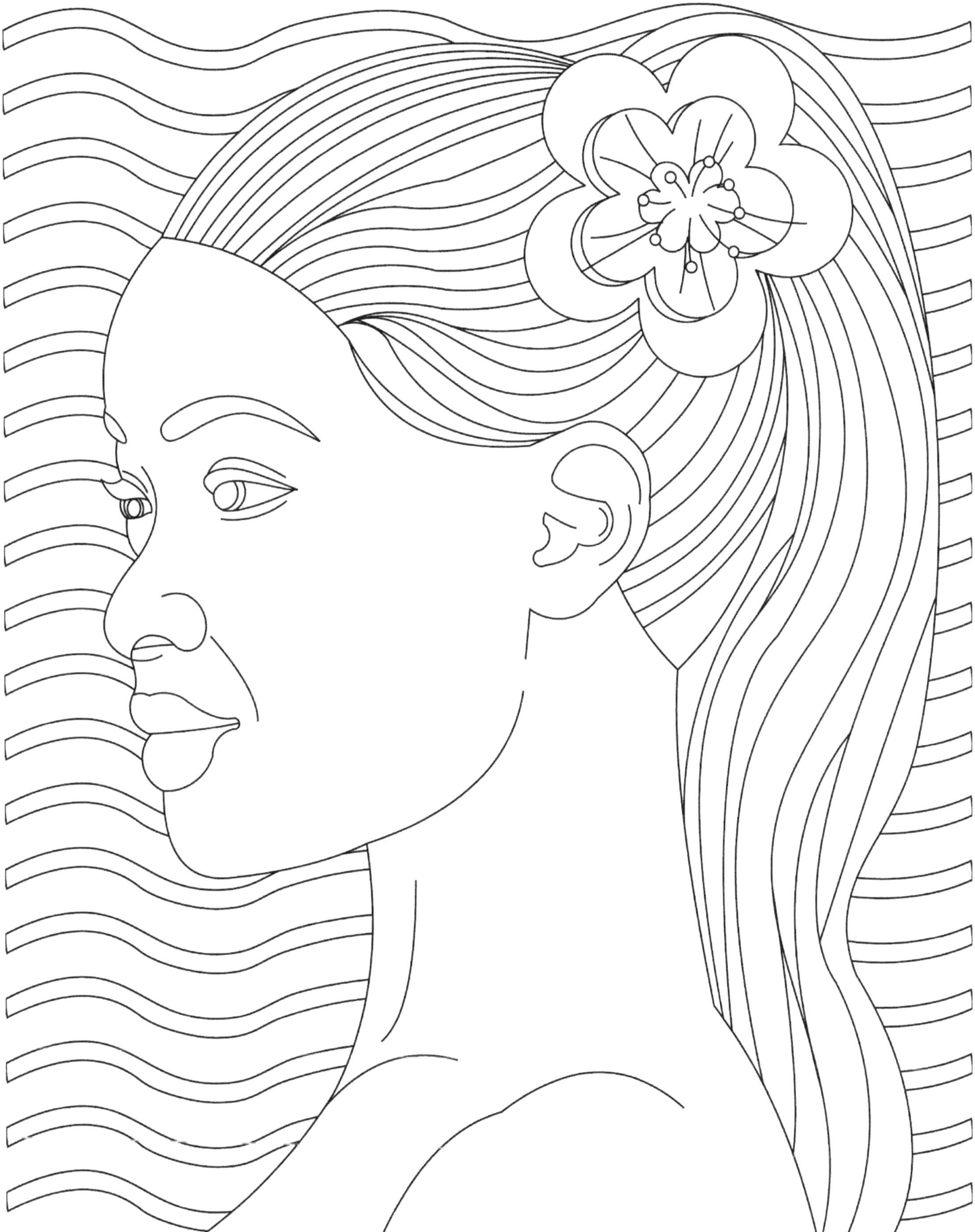

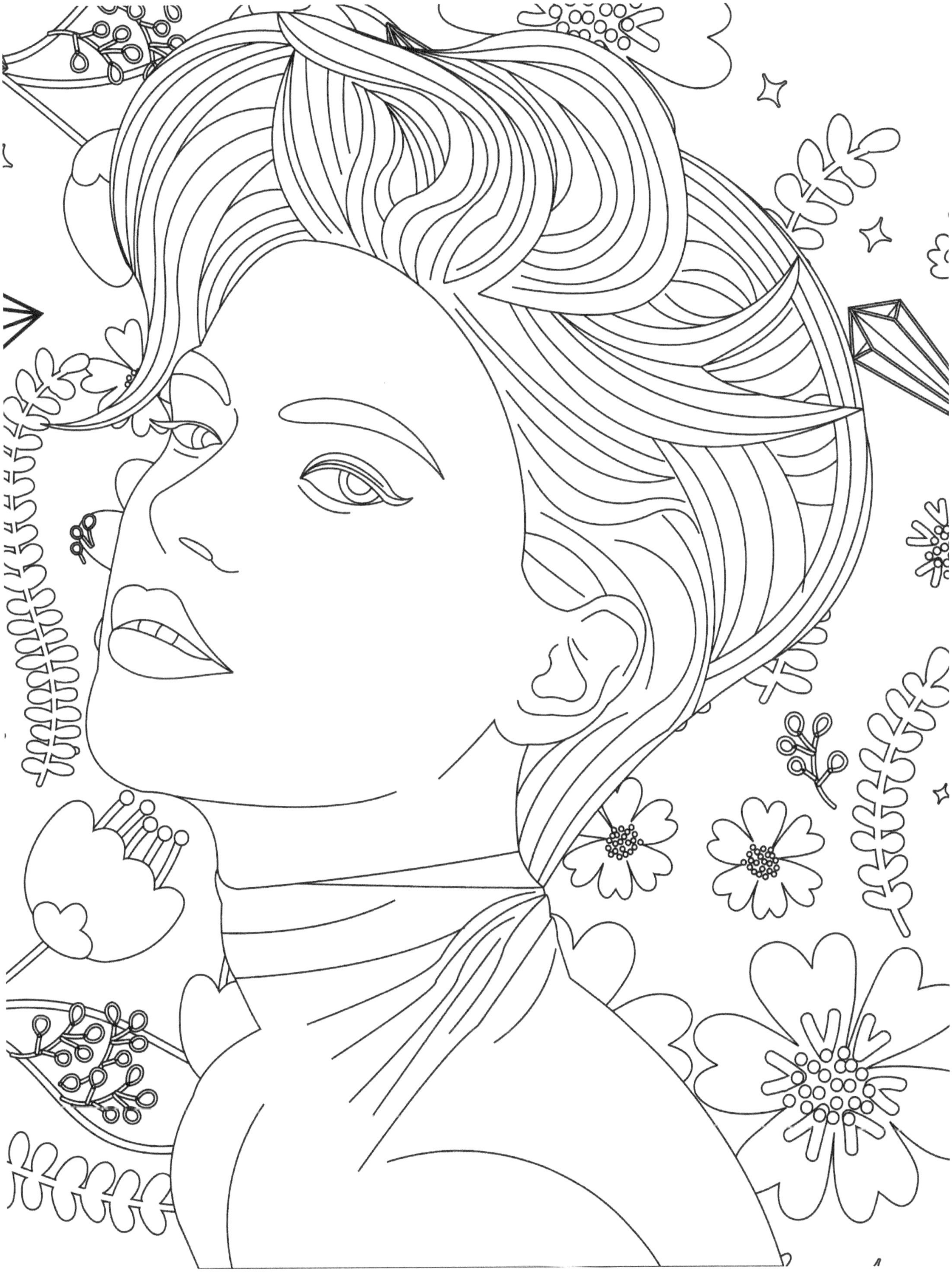

www.ingramcontent.com/pod-product-compliance
Lightning Source LLC
Chambersburg PA
CBHW080027260726
48658CB00007B/2499
*9781717172891*